Advance praise for

'An honest and poignant account... August 2021 in Afghanistan, which the world is still grappling with... What makes this book distinctive is the simple narration of an extremely difficult period that once again brought the Taliban back in power.'
     A.S. Dulat, former Head of Research and Analysis Wing and Special Director, Intelligence Bureau

'Nayanima Basu has given us a lively and informed account of her stay in Afghanistan at a pivotal moment, just as the Taliban took over the country in 2021. More than a diary of travel in a dangerous, exciting and exotic place, this book is an explanation of a phenomenon, the return of the Taliban, with which the world has yet to come to terms. Its consequences are still playing out, making this a valuable contribution to understanding the increasingly complex geopolitics of India's periphery.'
     Shivshankar Menon, former National Security Adviser and Foreign Secretary of India

'Nayanima Basu has penned a truly gripping first-person account of the dramatic fall of Afghanistan to the Taliban in August 2021. It reflects her indomitable courage in the face of acute and ever-present danger and her unfailing commitment to professionalism as a journalist. This is outstanding reporting but within a frame of deep political and historical familiarity with a truly complex country.'
     Shyam Saran, former Foreign Secretary of India

THE FALL OF KABUL

THE FALL OF KABUL

Despatches From Chaos

Nayanima Basu

BLOOMSBURY
NEW DELHI • LONDON • OXFORD • NEW YORK • SYDNEY

BLOOMSBURY INDIA
Bloomsbury Publishing India Pvt. Ltd
Second Floor, LSC Building No. 4, DDA Complex, Pocket C – 6 & 7,
Vasant Kunj, New Delhi 110070

BLOOMSBURY, BLOOMSBURY INDIA and the Diana logo
are trademarks of Bloomsbury Publishing Plc

First published in India 2024
This edition published 2024

Copyright © Nayanima Basu, 2024
Photographs copyright © Nayanima Basu, 2024

Nayanima Basu has asserted her right under the Indian Copyright Act to be identified as the Author of this work

All rights reserved. No part of this publication may be reproduced or transmitted in any form or by any means, electronic or mechanical, including photocopying, recording or any information storage or retrieval system, without the prior permission in writing from the publishers

This book is solely the responsibility of the author and the publisher has had no role in the creation of the content and does not have responsibility for anything defamatory or libellous or objectionable

Bloomsbury Publishing Plc does not have any control over, or responsibility for, any third-party websites referred to or in this book. All internet addresses given in this book were correct at the time of going to press. The author and publisher regret any inconvenience caused if addresses have changed or sites have ceased to exist, but can accept no responsibility for any such changes

ISBN: PB: 978-93-54353-48-2; e-ISBN: 978-93-54356-18-6
2 4 6 8 10 9 7 5 3 1

Typeset in Fournier MT Std by Manipal Technologies Limited
Printed and bound in India by Thomson Press India Ltd

To find out more about our authors and books, visit www.bloomsbury.com and sign up for our newsletters

Writing my first book was like giving birth to my son, Naume. I dedicate this book to him, in whom I see my parents – both my mothers (Sarmila and Mira) and both my fathers (Arunabha and Animesh).

CONTENTS

Map of Afghanistan		xi
Chronology of Key Events		xiii

1 Landing in Kabul and a Near Arrest: Welcome to Afghanistan! 1
   8 AUGUST 2021

2 Pounding the Streets of Kabul 19
   9 AUGUST 2021

3 In Mazar, as India Shuts Its Last Consulate and the Taliban Advances 31
   10 AUGUST 2021

4 Mazar, Free and Beautiful: The Taliban Did Not Run It Over 41
   11 AUGUST 2021

5 Kabul: Growing Eerier Day by Day 52
   12 AUGUST 2021

6 Has the Islamic Republic of Afghanistan Collapsed? 60
   13 AUGUST 2021

7 Mazar Gone; Can Kabul Be Far Behind? 76
   14 AUGUST 2021

8 Taliban Back in Kabul, and I Stranded on the Streets 87
   15 AUGUST 2021

CONTENTS

9   Will I Die Today?   112
16 AUGUST 2021

10   Back Home, with a Bit of Afghanistan in Me   129
17 AUGUST 2021

Epilogue   139

Acknowledgements   195
Notes   199
Sources   203
Index   209
About the Author   215

Map of Afghanistan

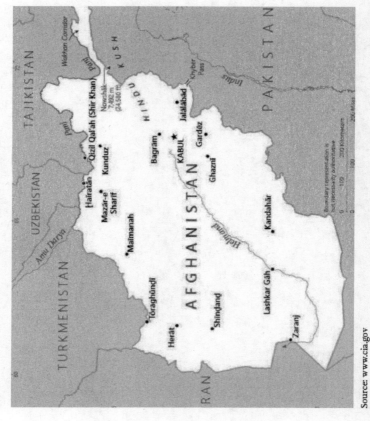

Source: www.cia.gov

CHRONOLOGY OF KEY EVENTS

1830 – Onset of the Great Game between England and Russia to expand their influence in Central Asia; eventually led to their confrontation in Afghanistan

1838 to 1919 – Three Anglo-Afghan Wars were fought as the British, who were ruling India, wanted to take over Afghanistan and eliminate Russian influence there (the wars were a direct result of the Great Game); the British finally gave up and signed a peace treaty in August 1919 recognising the independence of Afghanistan

1926 – Amir Amanullah Khan proclaims himself King of Afghanistan

1933 – Zahir Shah becomes the next king and rules Afghanistan for the next 40 years

1973 – Zahir Shah's cousin Mohammed Daoud Khan stages a coup with the help of the Soviet Union, abolishes monarchy and establishes the Republic of Afghanistan

1978 – Khan gets killed by Nur Muhammad Taraki, one of the founders of the Afghan Communist Party, who becomes the president as civil war rages on in Afghanistan with the creation of Mujahideen, a guerrilla movement, aimed at fighting the Soviet regime

1979 – The US severs ties with Afghanistan as their envoy gets killed, paving the way for the USSR to invade the country

CHRONOLOGY OF KEY EVENTS

1984 – Osama bin Laden, a Saudi citizen, appears in Afghanistan to assist the anti-Soviet fighters

1988 – Osama bin Laden creates Al-Qaeda to fight the holy war or jihad

1989 – Soviet withdrawal takes place; the US, Afghanistan, Soviet Union and Pakistan sign peace treaties in Geneva to accord independence to Afghanistan; civil war continues as the Mujahideen keep fighting the Soviet-backed regime in Kabul

1995 – The Taliban rises to power, promoting traditional Islamic values and Sharia laws

1996 – The Taliban, a Sunni Islamic fundamentalist and predominantly Pashtun movement, gains control over most of Afghanistan

1997 – The Taliban kills the communist president Mohammad Najibullah, who was under the protection of the United Nations (UN); Ahmad Shah Massoud's Northern Alliance comes to prominence for fighting the Taliban and its ideology

September 2001 – Massoud is assassinated on 9 September and two days after that, on 11 September, terrorists attack the World Trade Center towers in New York; the US blames bin Laden, who was then hiding in Afghanistan, for the attacks

October 2001 – The US and allied troops launch air strikes in Afghanistan as the Taliban refuses to hand over bin Laden to them; the decision was taken by the then US president George Bush

December 2001 – The Taliban is ousted from power and they go into hiding, abandoning Kandahar, their power centre; Hamid Karzai, an exiled Pashtun leader, is sworn in as the leader of an interim Afghan government

2004 – Afghanistan adopts a new constitution that calls for the equality of women

2005 – The first parliamentary elections are held

2006 – The war intensifies as NATO (North Atlantic Treaty Organization) expands its operation amid relentless fighting between the Taliban, Al-Qaeda and Afghan government forces

2011 – US forces kill Al-Qaeda leader Osama bin Laden; the operation was ordered by the then US president Barack Obama

2014 – For the first time, the US, under Obama, orders a gradual withdrawal of American forces from Afghanistan; NATO ends its combat operation in Afghanistan but troops remain to train the Afghan forces; Ashraf Ghani comes to power

2015 – Obama announces the continuation of 10,000 US troops in Afghanistan till 2016 and 5,500 till 2017 as his term comes to an end

2017 – US president Donald Trump plans to continue the presence of troops in Afghanistan; the US drops the 'Mother of All Bombs' on Afghanistan

2019 – Trump plans to invite key Taliban leaders to the US presidential retreat of Camp David but later cancels

2020 – The US and the Taliban sign a peace deal under which Washington vows to withdraw all troops by May 2021; the Taliban, on its part, promises to sever ties with terrorist groups and continue to participate in intra-Afghan talks for a permanent ceasefire

April 2021 – US president Joe Biden announces complete withdrawal of troops by 9/11

15 August 2021 – The Taliban comes back to power as President Ashraf Ghani flees Afghanistan, marking the collapse of the Republic

September 2021 – The Taliban announces a new caretaker government under Mohammad Hasan Akhund, a close aide of Mullah Omar, the founder of the group; Sirajuddin Haqqani, son of the founder of the Haqqani Network, is named interior minister, giving the dreaded militant group significant prominence

Landing in Kabul and a Near Arrest: Welcome to Afghanistan!

8 August 2021

It was a warm July morning and a Sunday, and like always I was preparing to catch up on my reading while also pondering on what news story I could file for Monday morning – the preoccupation of every daily news reporter in the country. As I lazily sipped my coffee, news started coming in from Kabul that India is 'temporarily shutting down'[1] its consulate in Kandahar. The Taliban at this time was gaining control of territory after territory in Afghanistan at a blistering pace. India's decision to shut down the consulate came as a shock to everyone, especially to those viewing developments in Afghanistan from outside the country. I thought something was amiss here. I started making frantic calls to my sources in the Indian government, who said the decision to shut down the consulate had been made because the situation in Afghanistan was 'highly volatile and fluid'. But the shutdown would be temporary and there was nothing to be alarmed about, they said. And this had been the government's line throughout that period of strife in Afghanistan. This also stemmed from the fact that India was heavily invested in the Ghani government and somehow had this blind faith that nothing could go wrong with it.

The establishment of a consulate in Kandahar had been a big achievement for India, considering that Kandahar was the birthplace of Taliban ideology and thereby a stronghold of the Taliban. India opened the Kandahar consulate after it resumed diplomatic ties with Afghanistan post the ouster of the previous Taliban regime in 2001. Of course, it was also the place where India's Research & Analysis Wing (R&AW) and Pakistan's Inter-Services Intelligence (ISI) were neck and neck in the race to gather intelligence and carry out their operations.[2] Up to as recently as April 2021, the consulate had been granting Indian Council for Cultural Relations scholarships to Afghan students,[3] and now, in less than three months, the Indian government had decided to shut it down all of a sudden. Despite the growing security concerns and clamour all around the world over the Taliban capturing vast swathes of land in Afghanistan and their rapid advancement towards its capital of Kabul, the Indian government continued to insist that the closure of its consulate was a temporary measure. Officially, it continued to hold that its consulate was still open. But to many, it was clear that India had indeed lost in Afghanistan, in terms of being in a position to gather intelligence for its counterterrorism measures against Pakistan.

LANDING IN KABUL AND A NEAR ARREST 3

Having four consulates in a war-torn country like Afghanistan was probably India's biggest strategic and foreign policy achievement, especially because it made Pakistan uncomfortable. All four consulates - Kandahar, Herat, Jalalabad and Mazar-i-Sharif were opened by India in 2001 after the first Taliban regime there came to an end. Islamabad had been waiting for such a day to come – when New Delhi would shut shop in Afghanistan on its own. Voices had already begun to emerge saying India was leaving too soon, and not moving fast would only change the plot against it. Strategy experts proclaimed that India's loss would be Pakistan's and China's gain.[4] And that was exactly what happened, as we saw in the days to come. The Western press, in the meantime, began running stories and analyses saying that Kabul's fall was only a matter of about six months. It was in June 2021 that the American press had begun to write that the Afghan capital would fall in the next six months.[5] By the time I reached Afghanistan in August that year, ninety days had already passed since that prediction.[6] So it was not just India, but the Western press too that did not read the writing on the wall right.

Not one to ponder over a decision once it was made, I told my editors that I wanted to visit Afghanistan. I was grateful that they permitted me to – and without asking me a single question. My editor-in-chief, Shekhar Gupta, had only this to tell me just before I left for Kabul, 'At any point if you feel overwhelmed, you can come back.'

Back home, my husband – a conflict photographer who covered Afghanistan in 2001 when the Taliban was ousted – was as excited as I was, if not more. My mother was extremely worried for me, for obvious reasons. But she had given up on me long back and knew it would be futile to even mention a word about stopping me. My only concern was for my little one, although for a nine-year-old he was an extremely smart and aware child. He has realised quite early in his life that his parent is not the quintessential mother eulogised by society, and I believe he has made peace with that.

Then began the process of obtaining a visa. I am grateful to then Afghan ambassador to India, Farid Mamundzay, and the press officer, Abul Azad Haq, for their promptness and understanding in this matter. They were appreciative of my passion to visit Afghanistan and report from there. While the embassy did not create any hurdles for me, getting a visa was nevertheless a long-drawn-out and tedious process. It was not easy for them to grant visas at a time when the headline news everywhere was about the imminent capture of Kabul by the Taliban. At the time, like the Afghan diplomats and the Indian government, I too was under the impression that these were just speculative stories and there would be a 'peace deal' between the Ashraf Ghani government and the Taliban leaders.

Meanwhile, tragedy struck. A promising photojournalist at Reuters, Danish Siddiqui, was killed in Afghanistan while on assignment there, and in the most brutal circumstances. But what shook everyone in the media industry was the fact that he was killed by the Taliban, which rarely targeted Indian journalists. While I had only heard about Danish from my husband and did not know him personally, I felt deeply shaken by what had happened to him because I was about to embark on a journey to that country soon. Never before had the Taliban ever killed an Indian journalist as their targets have mostly been Western media persons. So this was unprecedented, and it appeared that perhaps the Taliban would now also target the Indian media who had come to cover the withdrawal of US troops there. Indian journalists were still reporting from there; they were mostly from television, and mostly male. As the days passed, news started coming in from Afghanistan that the peace talks in Doha were gaining momentum. Doha, which still remains the de facto headquarters of the Taliban, was the venue for intra-Afghan talks that were going on at the time for the settlement of a power-sharing deal between the Republic of Afghanistan and the Taliban. These talks, taking place under US monitoring, were overseen by then US special envoy for Afghanistan, Zalmay Khalilzad, himself an ethnic Pashtun, who eventually had to step down from the post rather unceremoniously. In August 2021, Khalilzad's visits between America and Kabul increased in frequency as he was frantic to somehow get the power-sharing deal done so that Washington could justify its two-decade-long war there and now its withdrawal. Everywhere one could only hear one word, 'deal' – peace deal, power-sharing deal, etc. – while the Taliban was taking control of district after district and their masters in Doha giving a hard time to the US as well as to the Afghan government. Dr Abdullah Abdullah, who was the Ashraf Ghani government's chief negotiator of peace in the deliberations in Doha, had to face their wrath again and again, and while the world had pinned its hopes on him, he failed to work out a 'deal' with the Taliban. Two days before the takeover of Kabul by the Taliban, Abdullah, who held the official designation of chairman of the High Council for National Reconciliation, had reportedly made a power-sharing proposal to the Taliban. However, one refrain was constant through all of this – 'Taliban will soon take over Kabul'. While many laughed it off when they heard or read about it, in reality, it was indeed taking shape.

After waiting for more than two weeks, I finally got my visa for Afghanistan. It arrived on 30 July, a very wet day in Delhi, making it quite a task to reach the embassy to collect it, what with all the waterlogging near the Chanakyapuri area where it is located. It was all rather dull and gloomy, and for a moment, as I was driving to the embassy, a million questions swirled up in my mind, as well as the words of some former diplomats who discouraged me from going. But this was nothing new to me. People often refuse to understand the passion that drives a journalist; they think a journalist just exists to get press releases published in the papers. Some of them were genuinely concerned about my well-being and left no stone unturned to get me to change my mind. Afterwards, while I was reporting from there, some people, who never even for once appreciated my work or cooperated with me professionally, began inquiring me about my well-being while I was in Afghanistan almost every day. They were not concerned about my well-being at all but were just seeking out ways to stop me from reporting what was actually happening on the ground, which ran counter to their work on Afghanistan. They were upset that I was not writing the usual stuff that they wanted me to write. I was determined to report the unfiltered truth, which could not be digested by many back in India, especially those who run marquee think tanks. No surprise then that when I returned from Afghanistan they didn't bother to call me even once to ask about my experience there. In fact, none of the press clubs, including the press club dedicated to women, bothered to hear my story even once. But up to about six months after I came back I used to get calls from several of my readers, and women journalists working in the remote corners of the country called me to understand what it was like for a woman to do such an assignment.

But there were also those who encouraged me – among them a former R&AW officer who went that extra mile for me, giving me all the contacts he had retained from his days in Kabul and even putting me in touch with someone who arranged for my conveyance there. Then there were also those like former Foreign Secretary of India and former Chairman of the National Security Advisory Board (NSAB), Shyam Saran, who made it a point to call me over to his office at the India International Centre after my return and wanted me to share the whole story of my Afghanistan experience with him. I was grateful that CNBC TV18 and SheThePeople made an effort to discuss with me my experience there and what Afghanistan's future would be.

To come back to the day I received my visa, I reached the Embassy of Afghanistan in New Delhi's Chanakyapuri area through all that rain, and after waiting for an hour in the reception area I finally got it. For a few seconds I could not believe my eyes as I gazed at the words 'Visa Granted'. But I knew one thing for sure – I was unstoppable now. This was it! At that moment I could only visualise and hear my late father encouraging me to go to Afghanistan and give it my best shot. I was sure about one more thing – should something happen to me, he would be with me. I know this sounds rather odd and perhaps laughable, but when you know you are setting out on an assignment where anything can happen, all sorts of thoughts clutter your mind. I was, frankly, fed up with the 'Taliban coming' and 'Peace deal happening' reports that I was churning out sitting in my office in Delhi. And from day one I was clear as to why I was going there and what it was that I would be doing there. The answer to both was one – to do ground reporting. I was not going there to embed myself with the Afghan forces and send over some more images of bullets, bodies and boom-boom blasts that were cluttering the television channels and filling the pages of newspapers in India. I was a journalist, that too a female journalist, going there to report on what was happening, and I needed to do what would be remembered, which meant neutral reportage.

LANDING IN KABUL AND A NEAR ARREST 9

With my accommodation and air tickets booked, I geared up to pack my bags for Kabul while also preparing for the work I would do there. For a reporter working in digital media, there is never news-free time. A digital-media journalist is a completely different animal from one in the print or electronic media. This animal works for a 24x7 platform. News comes in from all directions, and you need to play the game really well. And with so much fake news floating around, it becomes all the more important for those in digital media to be absolutely accurate with their facts.

I made sure I met Ambassador Mamundzay for his advice, and he agreed to meet me for a brief time. He gave me some valuable advice that did help me later while in Afghanistan, which was indeed a dangerous destination to report from. He made sure that I booked into a 'safe' hotel where I would face 'less danger'; and by 'danger' he was not referring so much to the threat of the Taliban as the dangers I would face as an Indian journalist in Afghanistan on account of the Pakistani agents there. At this I became a bit sceptical, although this wasn't the first time that I had heard such statements.

Years back, in 2000, as a student of history at the University of Delhi, some of my classmates and I convinced our faculty to arrange for a visit to Pakistan to see some of the historical sites there, such as Mohenjo-Daro and Harappa. Luckily, the history faculty at Indraprastha College for Women (IP College) at the time was perhaps the best in the country, at least according to me. My professors were real torchbearers of women's empowerment and out-of-box thinking. They continue to inspire me profoundly. But even at that time some of the junior students from the history batch opted out of the trip as it was to Pakistan and they were told by their families they would not be considered eligible for marriage once they come back from that country. However, the India of those times was different from what it is now. Despite the two countries being fresh out of the Kargil War, we students were not harassed by any state-supported mob for undertaking a journey to Pakistan. Nevertheless, I did know at an early age what roaming around in enemy territory entailed. I knew long back what it meant to be followed by spies when you were an Indian travelling in an enemy country.

A former Indian diplomat who had served in Afghanistan during the mid-1990s clearly told me not to visit Kabul as he believed I would be kidnapped as soon as I landed there and perhaps even get raped. I had deep respect for him as he had given me a great deal of inputs for several of my reports, and his words that day left me greatly depressed. He even refused to share any of his contacts with me. But I did not allow myself to be deterred. Yet another diplomat, also considered an expert on Afghanistan, asked me if my husband supported me in this 'adventure' of mine.

Finally, D-day arrived. It was a Sunday, 8 August. I was overwhelmed by all kinds of thoughts and feelings. What if I did not make it back? What if I got killed? What would happen to my child? Would he understand that

LANDING IN KABUL AND A NEAR ARREST 11

his mother got killed while doing her job and following her passion, and not grow up thinking his mother was selfish? As I checked my luggage for the final time – it included four rare books on Afghanistan – I was also catching up on the news. That day the Taliban had overrun the northern Afghan cities of Kunduz, Sar-e-Pol and Taloqan.[7]

The harassment began at the airport in India itself. Never in my life had I ever faced a situation where my passport was taken away at immigration and I was made to wait, as if I was some kind of criminal running away from my country. The immigration officer asked me thrice why was I going to Afghanistan. And just as I guessed, he asked me about my earlier trip to Pakistan too. As if he had caught a criminal on the run, the immigration officer asked me, with one eye on my visa and the other on my face, 'Did you visit Pakistan?' I answered in the affirmative. By now his excitement had soared. Narrowing his eyes, he asked me the reason why. I answered in one word – Kartarpur. His excitement vanished in seconds, but he was not someone who would concede defeat easily. He left his seat to call his superior. I spent almost ten minutes in front of the kiosk before three officers entered the cubicle of the immigration officer and again and again checked my visas for Afghanistan and Pakistan. Not someone who could tolerate this kind of behaviour for long, I said the Pakistan visa was for covering the Kartarpur Corridor which had been inaugurated jointly by Prime Minister Narendra Modi and the then prime minister of Pakistan

Imran Khan. I explained to them that the Afghanistan one was for covering the withdrawal of NATO and US troops from there and that there was 'no link' between the two, as they were suspecting. In about two minutes I was given permission to proceed.

Inside the airport, everything felt surreal. This was my first trip abroad after the pandemic and the two big lockdowns in India, and my first time with Kam Air. As I was waiting to board the flight, I met many Afghan women and men and got chatting with them. They seemed completely unperturbed by what was going on back in their homeland. Some were happy to learn that I was visiting their country to cover the happenings there, some sounded sceptical and asked me what the need for my visit was since their country would be seeing the end of a twenty-year-long war. However, all of them seemed completely at peace, with an absolute sense of surety that the Republic would remain and that there would be a deal between the then Ashraf Ghani government and the Taliban. There was a sense of relief, especially among the older men – who were in their traditional attire and headgear – that the Taliban would enter mainstream politics as it had learnt its lesson and would make a power-sharing deal with the government in Kabul under a democratic setup, safeguarding the country's Constitution.

Among the Afghan passengers were women, men, parents, grandparents, youths and children. They displayed no fear and seemed excited to go back to their country. It is difficult to imagine how these very people must have felt to see their country undergo a complete change in the span of a week. Afghans have been coming to India for several decades, sometimes as refugees but most of the time for medical treatment and higher education.

The best part of the journey was the view of the Hindu Kush mountains.

When I landed in Kabul there was complete chaos at the airport – especially at the luggage and immigration counters. Somehow, Afghans turn into impatient and excitable beings whenever they come anywhere near an airport. It was very annoying to see them crowd around the immigration counters, jostle other passengers or pick up somebody else's luggage and just walk away. Their behaviour was generally rough.

Finally, after receiving a lot of curious glances and after some jostling on my own part, I managed to bring myself close to the baggage scanners everyone was putting their luggage into – all at once. It was like a competition, and everyone seemed to have planned to leave the airport at the same time. I was losing big time, so I geared up to join the competition. I put my backpack on top of all the luggage going in, only to realise seconds later that my laptop was inside it.

Just as I was tuning into that chaos, a man from nowhere picked up my backpack and began to walk away with it. I chased him down the exit, which was nearby, and took my bag from him, but not before he yelled at me. People there seemed angry all the time. Maybe this was the outcome of a prolonged war, I thought to myself. However, I later realised what the hurried rush at the airport was all about. There was always a sense of fear of war that lingered in the common psyche of the people. While centuries of wars had eaten away at their country like a moth, the Afghans were always scrambling for peace, in relentless search of a stable life.

I stepped outside and was immediately mesmerised by the freshness of the air. The bright August sun was out and a pollution-free wind was gently blowing in from the mountain ranges. My eyes fell on a vibrant signboard that said 'I LOVE [a heart sign] KABUL' . . . and instantly I felt connected with the land. Who would say this was a war zone, I told myself as I put my first step on Afghanistan's soil.

The walk towards the parking lot where my airport transfer was waiting was a long one and I enjoyed every bit of it. The land seemed free of any problems and I immersed myself in breathing the air, which had an untamed freshness to it. But as the taxi made its way into the city, the air changed; in fact, everything changed. There were tense faces everywhere and the air was heavy with something unpleasant, indescribable. It was all sinking in now, and for a second my son's smiling face flashed in front of me.

As is usual for me, I started up a conversation with the chauffeur, who seemed shocked to learn that I was from India. While he had been driving Indian journalists around, none had been female, he said. Most of them were TV reporters who had come to cover 'the war'.

LANDING IN KABUL AND A NEAR ARREST

However, he was happy to show me around, and for a short while I did not feel like a reporter sniffing for news but like a tourist trying to amalgamate into the surroundings as my taxi – a Toyota sedan – sped through the capital city. But as we drove deeper and deeper into the city, I began to sense the depression lingering in the air. This was nowhere a 'world-class' city, as some in Delhi had made me believe. The poverty, the blocked roads . . . the eerie sense of invisible eyes following you . . . grip you with unease. Kabul, at that moment, looked like something straight out of the pages of a historical dystopian novel, where everything seemed to be in an existential crisis.

I asked my chauffeur, who knew good English, 'Do you think Kabul will fall?' and pat came the reply: 'Yes, soon. But nothing to worry, ma'am. You enjoy Kabul.' Of course, I didn't expect to hear that, but just as I was framing my next question he asked, 'Will India give me a visa if I apply?', and there was palpable fear in his voice. I had no answer.

We then took a turn near the Arg Palace. The walls had monstrous portraits of the then president Ashraf Ghani, who would soon become a fugitive, former president Hamid Karzai and the legendary Afghan fighter Ahmad Shah Massoud. For a second these men seemed to me to be nothing but a bunch of narcissists.

There were men and children lined up the roadside begging for food; some people sold boiled eggs and bottled water to passers-by at the traffic signals. The traffic was reckless.

I tried to roll down the windows, but my driver warned me that someone could snatch my phone; and by someone he meant the children on the roads, who looked hungry but had such wonderful smiles on their faces as they ran around the pavements in their little phirans that they stole my heart the minute I saw them. Just as I was soaking all these sights in, the car came to a screeching halt in the middle of a busy road, and before I knew what was happening I was told I was under arrest.

We were stopped by the Afghan police, who looked like cops straight out of a Hollywood flick, dressed exactly like American soldiers, with helmets, well-fitted uniforms, goggles and night-vision glasses sitting atop the helmets in a fanciful manner. After a few minutes of altercation with my driver, one of the policemen began to shout at me and my driver began to tremble. I sensed that something really serious had happened. While the 6-foot-tall policeman was yelling at me in Pashto, which I was still learning (thanks to Google!), I could only make out one word – 'Pakistani, Pakistani!'

I shook my driver from the backseat so he could regain his mind and translate what the policeman was telling me. Of course, as a Delhiite, I was used to people yelling on the roads, but this was something beyond that – the policeman was pointing his AKM 7.62 mm assault rifle at me. My driver could finally muster up the courage to tell me that the policeman thought I was a Pakistani. That I was clicking photos near the 'sensitive' Arg Palace was proof that I was a spy. I was dressed in jeans and a shirt and had covered my head and upper body with a dupatta. There was nothing to definitively indicate that I was Indian.

The policeman asked me to delete the photos. I deleted two that he wanted erased and then told him I was a journalist from India. But he still kept looking at me angrily. I then said, quite at random, 'I am a fan of Shah Rukh Khan.' In seconds, to my great surprise, that fierce look turned into a smile and he let me go.

That was quite a smile!

In about 3-4 minutes I reached Kabul's famous, and probably the best hotel, Serena Hotel, which grabbed headlines days after the Taliban takeover when the then Pakistan ISI chief Faiz Hamid was photographed in a relaxed demeanour having an espresso. As I entered the hotel, I had to undergo four layers of checking. The last round included coming out of the car and then undergoing a thorough body check and then taking a long walk towards the reception. And one had to undergo this 7-minute-long security check every single time when one stepped out of the hotel. I followed each and every procedure diligently. Upon entering the hotel I was mesmerised by the massive lobby area which was then filled with foreign media crews. It seemed for a second that BBC, CNN, Al-Jazeera owned the hotel even as their reporters, cameramen and equipment were scattered all around.

As I checked in, I was asked by the lobby manager the duration of my stay. Since I was unsure, I told him it would be at least 20 days. He immediately asked me for the full payment for 20 days, which of course I refused, and I paid only for a week. I was carrying a limited amount of US dollars so I was careful not to spend upfront. I was not aware that none of the Indian banks were operational there so there was no way I could ask for extra money from my office if needed. According to the manager, it is a rule at the Serena to pay for the room tariff 100 per cent in advance as people tend to 'run away' from Kabul. In my case, I did not want to run away but stay back for a few more days.

I loved the room they gave me. It looked like a suite with a cosy study in one corner that helped me perfectly to write my stories or to do live video reporting. And the best part, the room had huge windows overlooking the crowded Froshgah Street filled with fruit juice vendors, kebab sellers and others. For the next few days this would be my nest.

2

Pounding the Streets of Kabul

9 August 2021

The morning began with the loud call of hawkers plying just outside the hotel. Many guests spent a bomb to live in the garden wing of the Serena Hotel in Kabul. My room was on the side of the hotel where the main road ran, but I considered myself lucky. I was told by a former Indian diplomat not to take rooms facing the road as there were chances of rockets being launched into the rooms. But this room allowed me to feel the pulse of the city, in whatever little way it did. The road in front of my room was noisy, but the hustle and bustle gave it the semblance of normality in a city living in the tight grip of fear and uncertainty. The man on the road, as in any other city in the world, seemed least concerned that the NATO troops would be leaving his country in a few days and that there were loud murmurs in every corner that the Taliban may soon capture Kabul. The war between the Taliban and the Afghan forces was intensifying too.[1]

I sat in the Serena's breakfast area and was quite amused that the black coffee I was sipping tasted perfect to me. I had managed to get my hands on one of Afghanistan's premium English dailies – *Afghanistan Times*. The first few pages were filled with news of the

Taliban obtaining complete control of the cities of Aybak and Sar-e-Pol and advancing on others.

The Taliban had also by then taken over Zaranj, the capital of the western province of Nimruz; Sheberghan, the capital of the northern province of Jawzjan; and Taloqan, the capital of another northern province of Takhar.

The Serena Hotel was also a favourite among journalists from the West, who were now filling the breakfast area and chatting about the rapid gains being made by the Taliban. While some were saying they needed to go back before their worst nightmares came true, others were planning to stay on. An American at a US-based NGO, who had been living in the hotel for many years now, overheard my conversation with another journalist friend and said nothing would happen before 31 August. I asked him what made him feel so confident about this, he laughed off my query; there was a tinge of superiority in his body language as he brushed away my question, as if he wished to add, 'Oh you silly Indian journalist . . .'

I firmed up my plans for the day, which included getting myself registered with the Indian embassy in Kabul, as that was what the Indian government advisory issued a few weeks before had recommended for Indian citizens there. Once I reach the embassy, I would be assured of help in terms of permissions and key contacts, I thought. If not news contacts, I would at least be recommended a reliable cab service to take me in and around Kabul. Conveyance in Kabul is a big deal. There are no cab-hailing services there, nor apps like Ola and Uber for foreigners. Unless you were a well-heeled journalist who travelled with bodyguards, you were sure to be targeted in some way if you got out on the roads and tried to get one. And the cab drivers could charge you just about any amount, and they only expected payment in dollars, I was told by a server at the Serena.

But for that day, thankfully, I had someone at my service, thanks to Anand Arni, former special secretary at R&AW and now a distinguished fellow of the Geostrategy Programme at Takshashila Institution. Arni helped me in every possible way he could before I started my trip. He connected me with someone whose cousin worked as a cab driver in Kabul. For years this man and his father used to drive cars for some of the embassies in Kabul.

I stepped out of the hotel and saw people thronging from one side of the road to another, as if they all had to make it to a concert. Another group of men came rushing out of the busy marketplaces around. The hawkers continued with their screams. For a second I thought they were all running away from some danger. I thought to myself, 'Has the Taliban taken over?' I checked my mobile, which was running on international roaming, for the latest news on Afghanistan, even though I had checked the news just before leaving the hotel.

In war zones, the situation can change in the blink of a second, and before you know it everything can collapse. I found out from some reliable Afghan news publications, which have an active presence on social media, especially Twitter (now X), that the Taliban had taken over the northern province of Sar-e-Pol even as the government forces ran away from there, or surrendered. So even as I began my work, I got a sense that the Taliban was fast closing in, as by then some of the key provincial capitals such as Zaranj, Sheberghan and Taloqan, and now Sar-e-Pol, were completely under Taliban control. Was Kabul really too far now?[2]

After a lot of difficulties on the road, which involved not just Kabul's infamous traffic jam but also mindless checking at some of the key checkpoints, I could make it to Afghanistan's Ministry of Foreign Affairs with the hope of meeting some of my sources, whom I had mostly been speaking to over the telephone from India. I also wanted to meet the then foreign minister Mohammad Haneef Atmar.

On his visit to India a few months before, in March 2021, the former foreign minister had boasted that the Ashraf Ghani government would call for early presidential elections and that Ghani was willing to transfer political power to the Taliban if they stuck to and expedited the ceasefire plan under the intra-Afghan talks. He had also called for greater engagement on New Delhi's part to deal with the Taliban. During his visit he not only met his Indian counterpart S. Jaishankar but also National Security Adviser (NSA) Ajit Doval. There were also talks on India's $3-billion development cooperation programme in Afghanistan and its implementation of projects across all thirty-four provinces of Afghanistan.

POUNDING THE STREETS OF KABUL 23

Just a month before his visit, India and Afghanistan had signed a memorandum of understanding (MoU) for the construction of the Lalander (Shahtoot) Dam on the tributary of the Kabul River to provide drinking water to Kabul city as well as irrigation for the nearby areas. This proposal continues to remain on paper.[3]

Interestingly, during this India visit, Atmar also met some of the former Indian envoys to Afghanistan, including veteran diplomats who had served in Afghanistan – Rakesh Sood, Vivek Katju, Jayant Prasad and Amar Sinha. Atmar, who was later seen in a video desperately running away to Turkey while his boss also fled to escape the Taliban's wrath, spoke about the 'will of the Afghans' and the so-called achievements of the last twenty years with the former Indian ambassadors.[4]

As I entered the Ministry of Foreign Affairs after three rounds of checking, I was made to sit inside a room that looked like one of those old post offices in New Delhi smelling of postage stamps and glue. But I would soon be actually writing letters there in order to obtain permission to get the coveted 'press card' from the Afghan government and also to see Atmar, who at the time was 'extremely, extremely busy', as one of his officers told me. As if one 'extremely' was not enough, he used the word twice, seeing the visible irritation on my face. However, the officer was generous enough to have a long chat with me, and our discussion ranged across many topics. He also wanted to know what I thought India's security situation was post the Galwan Valley clash between the Indian and Chinese forces in June 2020. The officer was more interested in 'China entering India' than in 'Taliban taking over Kabul'. The more I prodded him on the latter, the louder his laughter would become, as if I was cracking a joke and was a newbie journalist who had come to Kabul for 'having some fun'. He actually asked me to wander around in the city, relish some local cuisine, talk to 'progressive ladies' and enjoy the 'Kabul of today'.

As I made my way through the long corridors of the building, I met another 'close aide' of Atmar's, who expressed concern over my arrival in Kabul and was worried about me. But he said he was also quite thankful that at least one Indian journalist was making an effort to visit the ministries and get an assessment of the ground situation rather than getting embedded with the Afghan military and shouting 'War! War!' from a chopper high above the realities on the ground.

On my way back that day I found Kabul to be exceptionally quiet. The silence seemed eerie, but people were walking on the roads as usual and the markets were crowded. But the air was tense, as if in apprehension of some impending doom. I asked my cab driver if this was normal and if I was overthinking all this. He told me people were waiting for the Taliban to enter Kabul. 'Anything can happen any moment,' he told me.

Thereafter, I headed to the Indian embassy located in the heart of Kabul city. It's located inside a posh enclave that mostly houses all the important embassies and missions. The Afghan police personnel manning the

POUNDING THE STREETS OF KABUL 25

main gate did not have my car details, and showing my newly made press card did not help at all; I was turned back. However, the matter got sorted within hours and I could finally visit the embassy to get myself registered. At the embassy I was offered Afghan tea and the general mood inside was calm and relaxed. It seemed to me that the embassy officials were not quite happy with the fact that I was there. One of the senior officers in the embassy asked me in a jocular tone whether my intention was to become 'lady Danish'. I realised then and there that nobody within the embassy would offer any help to me, let alone good contacts for me to do human-interest stories. I wanted to interview Rudrendra Tandon, who was India's ambassador to Kabul at that time. I was told it will be done. However, matters changed so rapidly that I never got the opportunity.

After visiting the embassy I was somewhat relieved that nothing untoward was going to happen as the diplomats sounded absolutely sure of Ghani remaining in power. I made a quick detour to one of the women activists' home who gave me just ten minutes to meet her. Women activists in Kabul tend to be quite choosy and it takes quite a lot of hard work to get them to speak even one sentence. I reached her house which was near downtown Kabul and was awed to see her home. It looked like any other modern South Delhi house. She told me in clear words that the Taliban will overrun Kabul any moment and that I should make plans to go back to India. In a prophecy of sorts she also told me that she was concerned that the Taliban will prevent women from getting educated and it will be the same old Taliban. She even cautioned that this time the Taliban would be ably supported by the Haqqani Network and that would spell disaster for her country.

But back at the hotel the mood was dismissive of all this, as always. While having coffee with the American NGO worker I had met earlier in the Serena, I told him what the cab driver had told me. He laughed, as if I had gone mad. He told me, 'You Indians love drama, the reality is different.'

Nevertheless, I filed my news report based on the conversations I had had earlier in the day, and it went viral. I wrote a breaking story that the Afghan government had sought air power from India to fight the Taliban; if they failed to get it they believed the game would be over. But the thinking in India's foreign policy and security apparatus even at that time was that Kabul was not under threat and that a peace deal was near. Besides, it would have been a risky proposition to provide military support to Kabul and risk inviting the Taliban's wrath. But the bigger worry was that the Modi government kept its blinkers on when it came to the Ashraf Ghani government sitting at the Arg Palace. Many experts, former diplomats and former intelligence officials also held the same view, but for the Indian government to hold that line of view, at a time when it was working closely with the administration of the Afghan Republic, was foolish, I thought. The government was clearly unaware of the ground realities and failed to see the inevitable.

POUNDING THE STREETS OF KABUL 27

That evening I decided to step out of Kabul, no matter what, because reporting from the Serena was beginning to feel somewhat like reporting from Delhi, where one is able to hear only a select few voices propped up for the international media. I was fed up. I wanted to meet the people on the roads and decided to make good use of the so-called press card in the real sense. Chalking out my travel plans in my head, I stepped out of the Serena and proceeded to the nearby market, but nobody was willing to speak. Some looked irritated to see me, while some were willing to speak but didn't know Hindi or English. Thankfully, a passer-by volunteered to translate. He made me speak with a kebab seller.

The kebab seller, who had brown eyes, was extremely reluctant to speak to me. I asked him why, and his straight reply was: 'You are not BBC or CNN, you will not have dollars. I will speak only if you give me dollars.' This was immediately translated by the passer-by. The sheer honesty of these Afghans was beginning to impress me. There was no beating about the bush, no nonsense, just straight and simple business. But for me it was quite a shock! In India we still have free media, notwithstanding all the TV hysterics and digital activism, and we take pride – at least I do – in being the fourth pillar of democracy.

Nevertheless, I realised it was a war zone and there was no point talking about democracy here or giving them lessons in political science. So I asked how much he expected. He said $100 for speaking to him for fifteen minutes. I didn't have that luxurious sum to pay, so I politely refused. My makeshift translator began to laugh at this and told me that the kebab seller would not speak – but he did, for about twenty minutes, and then refused to go on further. I was happy because I got a glimpse, however small, into the life of a poor Afghan to whom it did not matter whether the Taliban came to power or someone else did. People like him needed just 'food', they needed 'peace'. And more than anything else, he was sure that the Taliban was coming. In fact, he asked me to stay safe as I was an Indian and the Taliban could be there any moment. He said, 'The Taliban does not like Indians.'

I tried to speak to some more people, especially the Kabuli taxi drivers, but neither I nor my translator could convince them to talk. They either wanted money or wished to speak into some fancy television cameras, I had neither. On my way back to the hotel, feeling rather let down, I gave my translator a few dollars. He was happy. While saying goodbye to me he told me, 'Madam, the Taliban are not someone who will come dressed as one, they are here among us. They are all around us. They have sleeper cells everywhere. There is Taliban among the staff in your hotel too.' Frankly, this was not the first time I had heard someone say that to me, but somehow at that moment it gave me the jitters.

Till late evening I kept thinking about what these two men had told me. Thanks to a kind-hearted manager at the Serena, I managed to get my hands on the last one

POUNDING THE STREETS OF KABUL

month's issues of *Afghanistan Times*. It was a paper provided to every customer at the hotel. I liked reading that paper every morning for its crisp and factually sound news and prescient op-eds. I read the papers till dinner time and realised one thing – it would be 'now or never', also the name of an Elvis Presley hit my father used to play every Sunday morning whenever he wasn't travelling for work.

With the help of a journalist friend, who was from a neighbouring country and whom I will always remain grateful to, my tickets to Mazar were booked and I packed my handbag for the trip, which was to be a short one. I was fully aware that I may not return alive because the Taliban was very close to the border of Mazar-i-Sharif. But sitting in Kabul made no sense as nobody was ready to open their mouths to speak and those who did belonged among the elite, who were least bothered about what was happening right outside Kabul's borders. Political biggies like Dr Abdullah Abdullah, and former Afghan president Hamid Karzai – who had promised to meet me and give me interviews – went silent. In fact, Dr Abdullah was dispatched to Doha in Qatar, where the Taliban has its headquarters, to coax it into a political settlement of sorts and to put an end to its military offensive.[5]

That night I called Tahir Qadiry, the ambassador of Afghanistan to Poland, to help me reconnect with the former governor of Balkh province, Ata Mohammad Noor, whom I had last met in New Delhi in October 2020 when he came to apprise the Narendra Modi government of the dangers lurking in the corners of Afghanistan and to ask for support in fighting the Taliban.[6] Ambassador Qadiry, who was then the chargé d'affaires at the Afghanistan embassy in New Delhi, had arranged for a small press meet with him.

Murmurs in Kabul were growing louder that Mazar would be the next to fall, so I wanted to visit the city before it became impossible to undertake a trip there. The kind-hearted person that Qadiry was, he vehemently discouraged me from undertaking a trip to Mazar at that time. A week before I left for Afghanistan, I had called up Qadiry and told him about my plans to visit Mazar-i-Sharif, the capital of Balkh province, and meet Noor. But little did we know then that things would come to this.

At dinner that night, I told a few fellow international journalists about my plan. All of them discouraged me from going to Mazar. The war was in its full intensity at the time. The Taliban was galloping towards the urban centres in the country, but somehow the world continued to believe that there would be a peace deal. As I called it a day, news came in that violence had escalated across large parts of Afghanistan and that Mazar-i-Sharif, Afghanistan's most important trading hub located on the country's border with Uzbekistan, was about to fall. Pul-i-Khumri was already gone.[7] I knew I had to carry a bulletproof vest. Kabul was full of international journalists at that time, so managing one was not difficult, owing to a few journalists who went out of their way to help others.

3

In Mazar, as India Shuts Its Last Consulate and the Taliban Advances

10 August 2021

After staying up all night as news of the Taliban entering Mazar-i-Sharif started gaining momentum on the international news channels, I quickly got ready for the airport. I had mixed feelings — on the one hand this was going to be *the* first frontline reporting I would be doing from a war zone, and on the other I was worried about my son and my family. But, as it turned out, my son was proud of me.

I got ready early and left for the airport. Kabul looked beautiful and inviting in the early morning, with its old-world charm and ruggedness. Everything looked quiet and serene, as if there had never been any Great Game played here. Entering the airport, I once again passed my favourite landmark signage there — 'I LOVE KABUL' — and made my way to the domestic terminal where people, mostly families, were lining up to go to Herat, Kandahar and Jalalabad.

At the security check-in, there were female checking personnel who were diligently scrutinising each and every item passengers carried. One of them checked the contents of my suitcase and asked the reason for my trip to Mazar-i-Sharif. Her blue-and-white uniform looked spanking clean and the name tag said 'Farkhondeh'. She had bluish eyes and reminded me of Steve McCurry's controversial 'Afghan girl'.[1] I told her why I was going, and she was stunned. She believed Afghanistan would see a 'new tomorrow' when the international troops left and become the true Republic that her generation had dreamt of. She was going off duty for that day and my flight to Mazar-i-Sharif was delayed by three hours, so we got time to chat a bit. I asked her if she thought the Taliban would take over Kabul. She laughed heartily and said that would never happen. She then left for home.

Looking out from the medium-sized windows of the domestic terminal of the Hamid Karzai International Airport (now Kabul International Airport), the mountains looked unfazed, as if they were telling the world 'enough is enough, leave Afghanistan alone'. These mountains must have seen the most bloodshed of any range in the world, I thought to myself.

Afghanistan has always been the world's most favourite battlefield. From Great Britain to Russia to the US, Afghanistan has been their famous playground to showcase their military and strategic might. But, in the end, all these three hegemonic countries turned out to be the losers; Afghanistan, or specifically the

Afghans, emerged as the winner. But this is one war zone where the party that wins continues to lose, as it has never been able to live a normal, stable life.

The British had fought three wars in Afghanistan, and every time it was defeated ruthlessly. General Frederick Roberts, infamously known as the conqueror of Kabul, had once remarked, 'The less the Afghans see of us, the less they will dislike us.' This prophecy was not off the mark as the British lost all three Anglo-Afghan wars, and it is no wonder then why the British and Russians', plans to invade have been called the 'Great Game'. All three wars that the British fought in Afghanistan (in 1838–1842, 1878–1880 and finally in 1919) were only aimed at one goal – thwarting Russia's advances and influence in the Central Asian region. For Britain, Afghanistan acted as a buffer zone safeguarding Russian advance towards British India.

Just as I was thinking all these things, I saw an elderly Afghan lady looking for a seat in the waiting lounge with her husband. She found one and quickly sat in it without wasting time and gave her handbag to her husband to hold. The husband stood beside her for the next two hours holding the handbag while she threw tantrums, possibly tired of waiting for their flight to Kandahar. Afghan husbands generally appear to be quite loving and family-oriented; not once during my entire trip there did I hear men yelling at or not taking care of their wives. But strangely enough, they believed in keeping their womenfolk indoors and did not have a modern outlook.

My flight got delayed for another hour and no information was provided. I wondered if Mazar had already fallen to the Taliban. Nevertheless, the mountains were too inviting for me to continue worrying for very long. For some insane reason, I thought – if I got killed in this land it would be an honour for me.

While a lot happened between the end of the third Anglo-Afghan War in August 1919 and the Russian invasion of Afghanistan in December 1979, it was during the Cold War between the US and Soviet Russia that Kabul got propelled to the centre stage of global geopolitics. This chapter in the history of Afghanistan would change the course of the world forever. While the Soviets did withdraw their troops in 1989, there emerged a second generation of Mujahideens who called themselves Taliban, or students of Islam.

The first generation of Mujahideens, or Islamist rebel fighters, came to prominence in Afghanistan when they fought to overthrow the Russian troops out of Afghanistan. But as the Russians left after nine years of rule, a new breed of Mujahideens took birth in the form of the Taliban.

Finally it was boarding time and my excitement knew no bounds. I boarded the Kam Air flight to Mazar-i-Sharif, and as the pilot said 'arm all doors', scenes of the Mazar-i-Sharif massacre that took place in 1997 began to haunt me. That was when the entire Balkh province had given a call to arms against the Taliban. It all started in the month of May 1997 when a massive revolt broke out between the residents of Mazar and the

Taliban over an issue concerning the minority Hazaras. In a matter of fifteen hours, the revolting residents of Mazar had killed some 600 Taliban fighters, who became easy prey in their hands as they were not well acquainted with the narrow and dark alleys of Mazar-i-Sharif. About 1,000 Taliban fighters were captured as they were trying to flee the massive bloodshed that was going on in the capital of the Balkh province even as summer was at its peak. The Taliban was defeated so badly that it was forced to recruit boys from the Ghilzai Pashtun tribes of eastern Afghanistan and Pakistan to defend itself. However, the tribes demanded something which the Taliban refused to give them. They wanted to clinch a power-sharing deal with the Taliban, which the latter rejected. This development exposed the Taliban's manpower shortage and recruitment hurdles.

As the plane entered Balkh province, the topography distinctly changed from what one saw in Kabul. There was less mountain and more barren land. There were vast stretches of desert as far as the eye could see. The airport was all barren and empty, and it appeared that mine was the only flight that landed there that afternoon. There were hardly a handful of passengers on that Airbus that day. While waiting at the baggage carousel for the bulletproof vest to arrive, for the first time on the trip, I met a man who handed over his 'business card' to me and struck up a conversation. The environment at Mazar airport that day had a certain eeriness to it, so I did not want to indulge him much, but he insisted on talking. He said he knew I was a journalist and that I was there to cover the 'arrival of the Taliban'. Seeing my passport, he began to sing praises of India, which quite impressed me. He called himself a 'fixer' and did not want me to report the events 'alone'. Obviously, he was trying to make me nervous so that I would 'hire' him as my tour guide, a common practice by foreign journalists, particularly Western reporters who visit Afghanistan to cover the place for a long period of time. As they heavily depend on these fixers they end up paying a hefty amount to them.

These so-called fixers in Afghanistan that I saw there have different ways of dealing with journalists from Western countries and those from South Asia and other places. He seemed like a kind man, but in war zones you cannot trust someone just based on your intuition. I took the gentleman's card and we left the airport as our respective baggage arrived. Stepping out of the airport one could see life-sized billboards of the former governor Ata Noor, wearing his famous Gucci glasses and staring out over a wide, semi-arid road right in front of the airport near the taxi stand. The billboards looked as if they were for some discarded Hollywood film.

I was fortunate to be connected with a cab driver – Osman (name shortened) – in Mazar-i-Sharif, thanks to a generous journalist friend. Osman also seamlessly and most efficiently played the role of bodyguard, keeping an assault rifle on the backseat. He also provided me with internet connectivity. He can also easily be called the world's fastest 'forex exchanger'. Without him my coverage of Mazar would have been woefully incomplete. He is an all-rounder, and I owe my coverage of events in Mazar to him. We have kept in touch. He tells me he is in the captivity of the Taliban. Since the Taliban entered Mazar, he says, the place has undergone a complete transformation, with no businesses running, no industries, no trading, and hence no jobs. People there are impoverished and are going hungry to bed daily. The Taliban has robbed poor families like Osman's by taking away their wives' gold jewellery, their savings and even a portion of their daily income.

Just as I boarded the taxi, I got the news that the Indian government was shutting down its consulate there, the last one to go after Kandahar, Jalalabad and Herat. I asked Osman to rush there, and he took me right to its doorstep. Unfortunately, despite my pleading with the Indian diplomat manning the consulate to meet with me, he refused to. He was busy preparing for the evacuation that was supposed to take place that night itself as the local authorities held that the Taliban would claim Mazar that very night.

Standing in front of the consulate, I video-recorded my report of what was happening. I then headed to the famous Blue Mosque, or the shrine of Hazrat Ali, where I met two of its head imams. The imams were generous enough to take me close to the sanctum sanctorum of the mosque and gave me a guided tour of the library and museum inside. I sat with them to discuss the situation in Afghanistan. I asked them if they feared that Afghanistan might again enter the dark ages if the Taliban took over. The two men were soft-spoken and polite, but firm in their conviction. One of them had a heavy baritone voice. He told me there was no scare, no fear, no worries among the people of an impending Taliban takeover. He gestured with his hands towards the main courtyard of the mosque and said, 'There is Taliban everywhere.'

'What is Taliban? They are students. Why is the world so scared of God's students?' he said.

He took me outside to the courtyard and showed me around. He asked if I could differentiate between a common Afghan and a member of the Taliban. Then he asked me if I could differentiate between a common Afghan and an American. 'Who is the foreigner? You will know. Taliban is our own. What have the Russians given us? What have the Britishers given us, what has Karzai or Ghani given us? What have the Americans given us? Let them [the Taliban] also have their chance.'

As I made my way out of the mosque, I did a small video story to convey the mood of the place, standing on the road leading out from the main chowk of the mosque. As I began to record my report, people on the road started to encircle me slowly and began threatening my driver. They were upset that I had a bulletproof vest on and they wanted me to take it off because they did not feel any war was going on. My appearance in that vest at the city centre would make it appear that there was tension in the area, and they did not like that. So I had to take it off and continue my reporting. Meanwhile, a frail-looking Hazara man from the crowd began yelling at my driver, saying that if we did not move out from there in the next ten minutes there would be 'consequences'.

IN MAZAR, AS INDIA SHUTS ITS LAST CONSULATE 39

I had to cut short my shoot, and as it was getting dark my driver urged me to head straight for the hotel.

I was told it would be safer to check into a hotel before the sun set. I was booked into Arsalan Guest House – a nondescript motel on the outskirts of Mazar-i-Sharif. Located in a tiny neighbourhood, with apartments no taller than three or four storeys sharing a common wall with the hotel, it felt like I was in a rundown inn in rural India. But the staff was warm and hospitable – so warm that after my check in they gave me a straight five-minute lecture on what do to 'if' the Taliban attacked Mazar that night and captured it. I heard them patiently even as my mind raced and I thought of my son, my husband, my brother and the whole bunch back in India. Most importantly, I thought of my mother and whether she would be able to absorb another shock after my father's death just a few years back. My grandparents were long gone. All my life I had seen her absorb that immense pain of losing her parents, but would she be able to move on if something happened to me? Anyhow, I heard out the staff as they described the 'survival plan'. They said I could be saved from the Taliban if I ran into their 'iron room' on the topmost floor should they 'attack tonight'. Not one to accept directions easily, I asked the brave hotel boy how I would know if the Taliban had indeed 'attacked'. He replied, 'Oh, don't worry, we shall call you on the intercom!'

Food is never a problem in Afghanistan for non-vegetarians like myself. If nothing else you will get meat in some form. And if you are a Bengali, like me, you have nothing to complain about in the matter of food. So, dinner was done and I locked myself up in my 600 square foot room that night, surrounding myself with wires and plugs on the bed and focusing on my writing, but with the intercom kept far away. There was no television in the room, which had only a bed, a half-broken mirror and a rickety wardrobe. The attached bath had just the bare minimum of attachments. But the internet connectivity was perfect and high-speed! As I worked, I kept checking the news. Soon, every international news channel started reporting that Mazar had fallen. I called the hotel reception at 1.30 a.m., 2.15 a.m. and 3 a.m., but there was no answer. Finally, at 3.10 a.m., someone with a heavy voice answered my call. My heart sank, thinking it must be a Taliban fighter, very much as in the Hindi movies, where a Taliban-type character can only have a heavy, masculine voice. For a second I wondered if I should make a dash for the 'iron room' or first do a short interview with him.

I asked him who he was. He said he was a cook in the guest house. Relieved, I asked if the Taliban had indeed taken over Mazar-i-Sharif. He denied it. I told him what the news channels were saying; he laughed heartily and asked me to check for myself by going to the city square. I kept the phone down and dozed off for an hour.

4

Mazar, Free and Beautiful: The Taliban Did Not Run It Over

11 August 2021

I woke up at 5 a.m. to see a thin streak of golden sun rays falling on my laptop. For a second it felt like my father was standing there and was in the room with me. I realised that I had got yet another day to live. I could hear the sound of choppers hovering in the skies. Something big was about to happen. Suddenly, the doorbell rang. A tall, thin man with spooky eyes was standing outside the door with my breakfast. He smiled and handed over the tray to me. I was not expecting room service in this hotel.

Meanwhile, I started calling my sources and found out that President Ghani was coming to Mazar that morning to meet all the leaders of the erstwhile Northern Alliance – the anti-Taliban rebel group – to discuss the next steps as Abdullah was out in Doha clinching the last leg of the peace deal. This seemed weird, because on the ground the Taliban was progressing towards Kabul at a blistering pace, but somehow people there were living in the hope that as the US began its final withdrawal everything would be 'settled', as my driver later told me. Everyone that day seemed excited that the Taliban's effort to take over one of the busiest trading hubs in Afghanistan would be effectively thwarted.

The day brought with it some glimmer of hope, and it seemed a transition government was in the making. But already, over the last week, the Taliban had seized nine provincial capitals. Mixed opinions were coming in from all quarters.

As soon as Ghani landed in Mazar, he met Noor, Abdul Rashid Dostum, a former vice president who was once a key leader of the Northern Alliance, which had fought the Taliban back in the 1990s, and Hazara strongman Muhammad Mohaqiq. I spoke to Noor's elder son, Khalid Noor, who told me that the Northern Alliance would be strengthened, Mazar saved and the Taliban pushed back from there. It all sounded too good to be true. Whatever might be the final outcome, I thought, I had got a blockbuster story for that day, and nothing else mattered to me.

Meanwhile, in an interview with the news channel Al Jazeera, Afghan interior minister, General Abdul Sattar Mirzakwal, said the Taliban should 'stop their brutality ... leave the killing, sit down with love and we should find solutions. I'm asking them not to destroy buildings, or our achievements'. He even admitted to the government having lost control of key roads and highways and the limited air support it had.

I started my day by gearing up to leave for the frontline, but my main aim was to interview General Noor and understand from him what was really happening in Afghanistan and if the Northern Alliance really had it in it to take on the Taliban.

This was not just any war frontline. The Pul-e-Bukhari area on the outskirts of Mazar city was once a village bustling with activity. But today the houses there, which once had residents and were full of life, lie charred and look haunted. At that time the Pul-e-Bukhari area was witnessing intense fighting; it was regarded as the last entry point to central Mazar, which the Taliban was hell-bent on claiming. I met a group of fifteen to twenty young soldiers there who were willing to go to any extent to 'eliminate the enemy . . . the Taliban . . . the Pakistani'. Soldiers are expected to be energetic; soldiers are expected to fight valiantly without caring for their own lives. But these were not ordinary soldiers. These young men – some of them perhaps still teenagers, the eldest being only twenty-three – said the Taliban was from the dark ages and would ruin everything that Afghanistan had gained over the last twenty years while the American war was on. I asked them if they want the war to continue; they said they were willing to face anything but would not have the Taliban ruling them.

These youth thought their government would help them, sending reinforcements soon so they could win the war against the Taliban. Little did they know at the time that their President was gearing up to run away from the country 'like a coward' as a former Afghan minister later told me. But that day was different. Their President was in town, and so they fought with greater zeal. They told me they hadn't been paid their full salaries for nearly two years and hadn't been given time off duty to go home for more than a year now. And yet there they were, in this godforsaken vast stretch of semi-desert land, fighting the Taliban day and night.

In an address to the Oxford Union almost nine months after he and his government fled from the country, putting an entire nation of over 40 million on the brink of collapse, Afghanistan's former NSA Hamdullah Mohib had the gall to boldly claim that his government had paid the Afghan soldiers 'until the last day of the government', which he said had collapsed because there was 'no unity of purpose'.[1]

At Pul-e-Bukhari that day, there was an air of jubilation. The Taliban had been pushed back, although the fighting was intense, and whispers of a revived Northern Alliance were gaining ground. It seemed that somehow everything would be fine. I sat with one of the young soldiers inside a run-down tank from which they were shooting at the Taliban fighters who were hiding in the faraway grasslands. As the tank moved, hunting for Taliban fighters, we passed burnt houses that looked like they had people living in them in the not-too-distant past, a dilapidated eatery with posters of kebabs still hanging, several charred tanks and vehicles. I asked if there were any soldiers who were killed inside these vehicles, and he answered in the affirmative with a kind of guilt in his eyes, which welled up as he dwelt on the fate of his buddies inside those vehicles torched by the Taliban.

MAZAR, FREE AND BEAUTIFUL 45

This, undoubtedly, was one of the most difficult events I had ever reported in my life. I was covering a war that was unstructured, uneven and completely unconventional compared with the Russia–Ukraine war, which is more planned and structured, and I was reporting it alone. In the case of the Russia–Ukraine war, there are professional armies fighting the war on both sides. They have a strategy in hand to follow and they know their enemy well. But in the case of Afghanistan, soldiers in the Afghan forces were not properly trained and there was no war strategy as NATO had almost left by then. And, most importantly, they did not know how many Taliban were there.

Some of my readers and viewers were sending me DMs (direct messages) on X advising me to also thank my cameraperson-colleague, but little did they know that my colleague had been denied a visa by the embassy and that I was doing everything single-handedly. People were comparing me with Clarissa Ward of CNN and some other women journalists who were also covering Afghanistan. Again, little did they know that I had absolutely no manpower support. While at times all this made me feel depressed and exasperated, looking back now I don't regret that I was alone at all. It greatly gave me confidence in myself as a multimedia journalist, and in my ability to report in any circumstances, something even my male counterparts cannot fathom to this day.

As I bade the young soldiers farewell, we shot selfies and some of them even shared their WhatsApp numbers with me. They said they would like to visit India and see the Taj Mahal. One of them wanted to meet his mother just once wearing 'American style uniform and goggles'; he was planning that for December. Two days after I met them, on the night of 14 August, the Taliban captured Mazar and I got to know from my local sources there that all the soldiers who were manning the border in the Pul-e-Bukhari area had been killed in an ambush. The Taliban unfurled its flag at the same point in the middle of the city centre from where I had reported just a few days back.

Finally, I got a call from General Noor's office informing me that he was willing to give me an interview. It was an opportune moment for the interview as General Noor had just met President Ghani a few hours back, along with other key members of the Northern Alliance. The entry to his house was not at all what I had expected it to be. I thought it would be palatial, with a big compound full of big-bodied men, but it was a small village home with several barriers in front. When I arrived at the compound of his main office, I was subjected to a rigorous checking, which involved a lion-sized dog. For a second I felt like dropping the idea of interviewing him, I have never been a great fan of canines. Nevertheless, I emerged unscathed from the checking and I could enter his office, which was as ornate as it could be. For a moment it seemed I had stepped into a fantasy world. His office-cum-residence reminded me of the Saudi king's office which I had visited in 2019, resplendent with gold-lacquered staircases and ornate sofa sets.

Noor made a grand entry with his men, wearing his signature Gucci shades and an enormous black tourmaline ring, which he wore on one of his right fingers. But this time he was not wearing a suit, as he had when I last saw him in Delhi, but army combat fatigues. He was accompanied by his two sons and was surrounded by his trusted men, all in combat fatigues as they could be called to the frontline any moment. They were all carrying rifles and grenades. The interview went on smoothly, his elder son translating the interaction. However, there was palpable tension in the air. During the interview General Noor once again appealed to the Indian government for more support, especially air support. With the US and NATO troops withdrawing from Afghanistan, the Afghan government had become weak in air power, he said.

As the interview was being wrapped up, Noor told me that he would defend Mazar to the end. Noor is quite a popular figure among some of the veteran Indian diplomats who have served in Afghanistan. Noor had fought for and saved the lives of Indian diplomats when the Indian consulate in Mazar-i-Sharif had come under terrorist attack in January 2016, following a deadly assault on an air base in India near the Pakistan border. So he has considerable goodwill within the Indian government, and his suggestions, opinions and inputs on Afghanistan are given a lot of weight in India. Noor said he expected India to assist the Afghan government in the ongoing fight and not 'forget' Afghanistan.

Leaving his residence, I felt that nothing was that hunky-dory after all. Noor had sounded much more concerned this time. He did not sound very enthused about resurrecting the Northern Alliance either. I wound up my work in Mazar and made my way to the airport to return to Kabul. I was booked on Kam Air again and was not feeling very tense because this was one airline known not to cancel flights even if there was impending danger. I reached the airport four hours before my flight. By now I had also learnt one thing about Afghanistan – the airports are always crowded and nobody follows any rule. Just as I expected, there was a massive crowd at the airport. I thanked my driver, an all-rounder, for his tremendous help and cooperation. He smiled and said, 'Wish I could come to India with you. Here life has no guarantee.'

The airport was teeming with millions of Afghans, 90 per cent of whom were 'running away' with pots and pans and everything else they could lay their hands on, all tied up in huge bedsheets. They were leaving their homes in search of greener pastures in Kabul, and then, if luck went well, perhaps to some foreign land from there. I met one such family of twelve, fleeing Mazar-i-Sharif to join their father in Turkey, who worked as a chef there. They were booked on the same flight as mine, and while checking in their baggage the whole family shoved their suitcases, bundles and bags in front of me and blocked the entire queue as if only they would travel and none of the others. Not one to tolerate this kind of behaviour easily, I confronted them and made

MAZAR, FREE AND BEAUTIFUL 49

them apologise. I realise now that they were escaping the Taliban, running for life, so nothing mattered to them. But I was also tense in that situation, seeing the airport filled with people, with no queues, with almost nil airport security personnel. After everything was done I found out that the flight to Kabul was running seven hours late!

That evening, flights from Mazar-i-Sharif to every other destination took off but not the last flight to Kabul. Rumours began to spread thick and fast that the Taliban had entered Mazar and would soon capture the airport, which was why no flights would now take off or land. As time went by, everybody started to panic. Some said the Taliban had locked the airport from the outside so that no one could enter or exit. Gradually, the entire waiting lounge of the airport, which somewhat resembled the old Ahmedabad airport, became empty and only the passengers for the last flight to Kabul were left, waiting with bated breath for some announcement. Mr. Gupta was with me on the phone constantly, calling me every thirty minutes to ask about my flight status.

Suddenly someone in the crowd shouted to say a flight had landed, but nothing could be seen. Everyone was asked to huddle up in a corner of the waiting terminal. I sat near a group of young girls, twenty-somethings, who asked me if I was from India, and when they learnt that I indeed was, their next question was whether I had seen Shah Rukh Khan and Deepika Padukone. Just to keep their hearts warm, I lied. I said I had met both. Thus started our conversation. One of them – Zarmeena – asked me why India shut its consulate in Mazar. Her words shake me to this day. She said, 'Why did India shut down its mission in Mazar? Nobody threatened you, we all love you and your country. Now that your mission is shut, we feel like our closest friend has deserted us. This is the reason why we are also running away.'

Zarmeena had plans to visit her aunt in Kabul and then apply for an Indian visa. Her dream was to pursue higher studies at Amity or Sharda University. She was fleeing Mazar with her two brothers, their wives and a widowed mother. The brothers planned to stay in Kabul as they believed that was a much safer place than Mazar. They felt the Taliban 'would not dare' to come to the borders of the Afghan capital. Another couple sitting silently in the corner asked me if I needed a translator/fixer in Kabul. Married for two years, the couple was expecting their first child and so they were running away to Kabul, a 'safer destination', away from the Taliban's atrocities. We exchanged numbers and the wife asked if I knew anyone who would give her the job of a domestic help. She was a teacher by training. Her request sounded heart-wrenching to me, and I wondered if Kabul would be able to give these people the protection they were all hoping for.

The flight finally arrived, way past midnight. The gates opened and the boarding was completed in exactly twelve minutes. It was a full flight and everybody looked jubilant as the plane took to the air. We landed in Kabul at 3 a.m. Exiting the airport, I once again ran my eye over the 'I LOVE KABUL' signage and once again inhaled the fresh breeze gently flowing from the mountains surrounding the airport. Having not eaten the whole day, I felt dizzy. Upon arriving at the Serena, I ordered a burger, which was served in less than fifteen minutes. Despite being a war zone, Afghanistan never failed in hospitality.

5

Kabul: Growing Eerier Day by Day

12 August 2021

This is a day I would never want to see again.

An uneasy calm hung over Kabul since the morning. I felt restless, as I used to even at home when I did not find a story to file. I stepped out of the hotel for a bit, only to find myself again in the midst of a meaningless crowd just walking to and fro aimlessly. And everyone seemed scared. I wanted to speak to people, but my attempts were of no use. So I returned to the hotel. I also wanted to have some time to myself. Covering a war zone is not easy, and some days feel heavier, especially the relatively calmer days. But journalists do not have the luxury to sit back and relax, so mentally I was still searching for stories.

All appointments and meetings with senior government officials kept getting cancelled and all their key aides started to go phantom. I kept pushing for an interview with Abdullah, which was promised by his team before my trip. I was told I would get one as soon as he was back from Doha. Reports from the Qatari capital were not sounding very positive as the peace talks with the Taliban had almost collapsed and prospects of a power-sharing deal looked grim. And all the while the Taliban was claiming provincial capitals and cities, one after another.[1]

Back on ground zero, the Taliban took over Ghazni, and that literally shook Kabul. I knew something was amiss when some of my sources in the Kabul government told me they were packing their bags, while some sought my assistance to secure a temporary Indian visa before they could make their way to the West. But how could I have told them that I myself was unsure of getting any help from the Indian embassy there if the Taliban took over Kabul? I was being constantly told by the mission that there was no evacuation happening. It was only when the actual exercise took place that I realised it was incorrect on my part to blindly believe them. The embassy, I learnt later, had been in evacuation mode since 14 August, after Ghani fled from the country.

The then US chargé d'affaires in Afghanistan, Ross Wilson, was quoted as saying, 'The Taliban's statements in Doha do not resemble their actions in Badakhshan, Ghazni, Helmand and Kandahar . . . Attempts to monopolise power through violence, fear and war will only lead to international isolation.' Wilson and his team at the embassy in Kabul had sent a dissent cable on 13 July 2021 warning of a possible takeover of Kabul by the Taliban.[2]

The conquest of Ghazni, which was the tenth provincial capital that gave in under Taliban pressure, was the easiest task for the Taliban as its then governor

Daoud Laghmani simply handed it over to the Taliban forces. Subsequently, he was arrested by the Afghan government in the outskirts of Kabul. The city of Ghazni had been under the Taliban forces for several months and the Afghan government had been controlling only the provincial office and a few governmental facilities.[3] Now those fell too.

Kabul was abuzz with murmurs that President Ghani was stepping down from his post. The Afghan army was falling like a pack of cards, and Afghans in Kabul, inside university campuses, hotels, restaurants, salons and markets, were saying the Taliban could enter the capital city any moment and there was nobody to defend it. Those who had the money for it were already hunting for air tickets to flee the country, calling their relatives in the US, Europe, Canada and Australia to make place for them and arrange for jobs and permits for them there.

It was a strange environment that day in Kabul. People I knew and called friends . . . nearly all were packing their bags to leave. Some still had faith in the Afghan government, while some – and they were the educated class who worked with the former government – wanted to give the Taliban a 'second chance', should it govern in a democratic manner. This felt strange to me. Back home in India, the news on Afghanistan suggested there was total chaos in the country. My family was beginning to worry for my safety, and by now my mother had completely given up hope about me. Had it not been for my husband, my mother would have had a nervous breakdown.

But to me, sitting in Kabul, the city appeared completely peaceful. It was calm and serene and people seemed to already have their respective Plan Bs ready. I guess this is what it means to be truly resilient – where you don't panic, don't get nervous, but silently make your escape plans. However, it is also true that while the upper middle class, the rich and the elite of Kabul had a Plan B, for the poorer lot it was a 'do or die' kind of a situation. Like all the poor in this unfortunate world, they were helpless. But for the poor of Afghanistan, it also meant having a government that would be proscribed by every country as well as the UN. And being ruled by a banned entity meant having restricted access to food and basic necessities of life, living in perpetual poverty.

Once again, to get a sense of the pulse of the people, I reached out to the lady in the salon, the waiters in the Serena and my cab driver, asking them what it would mean for them if the Taliban came knocking on their door. They were very clear, almost with a sense of surety, that this would not be the Taliban that had ruled earlier, from 1996 to 2001. They argued that this Taliban would know that they were coming back in a changed Afghanistan, a modern-day twenty-first-century Afghanistan where women and men were bold, beautiful and hardworking, knew what they wanted and whom they wanted to rule them, and would not give in to any kind of suppression. The gun did not scare them any longer, nor the bombs, and they knew they would be successful in asking the Taliban to have a democratic government. Somewhere deep in their minds they still nurtured the hope that there would be a 'power-sharing deal', a 'peace deal', that would come of the intra-Afghan talks that were still continuing in Doha.

Meanwhile, the lights in Doha continued to turn dimmer and dimmer. After a rigorous two or three days of talks, they finally ended that night with no tangible outcome in sight even as the Taliban continued to gallop across the north, south, east and west of Afghanistan and seemed very near Kabul. It is no wonder that the US, China and a handful of other countries urged the Afghan government to close the talks and wrap up the peace process as a 'matter of urgency'.[4] The much-touted intra-Afghan talks, fanned by the Americans as the next step following the peace deal, seemed to be crumbling fast.

The intra-Afghan talks began six months after the US-led peace deal was signed in September 2020 at the luxurious Sharq resort in the Qatari capital. Back in Kabul after the Doha talks, President Ghani and his man Friday, NSA Mohib, started chalking up plans for their own evacuation from the country, hoping Washington would lap them up. It would eventually turn out that two days later, on 14 August, when President Ghani addressed the nation, Mohib came to know that a colleague of his at Arg Palace had received the green signal from the US embassy in Kabul for his evacuation from Afghanistan. He immediately called up an acquaintance in one of the US State Departments under the pretext of discussing the peace talks, but his ultimate motive was to find out what evacuation plan the Biden administration had drawn up for him and for Ghani. Not very happy with the lackadaisical response from the US, Mohib also reached out to the UAE, which promised him and Ghani safe evacuation via an executive jet.[5]

The Taliban seemed to be on a rampage from this day onward. It claimed it had brought under control the provinces of Herat, Ghazni and Kandahar. While Ghazni and Kandahar were actually under its control, Herat was difficult to bring to heel as the regional strongman there – Ismail Khan – put up a massive fight against the Taliban. He was captured by the guerrillas the following day.

Meanwhile, I was busy catching up on some international news. My hotel had practically every major television news channel, but for some reason that day not all the channels were being aired. Upon inquiring I found out that the hotel was shutting down some of the transponders. It appeared that an information blackout of sorts was slowly taking place. Oddly enough, the salon inside the hotel was shut. I sensed something was wrong.

That day an art exhibition featuring works by local artists was going on in the ground-floor corridor leading to the main entrance of the coffee shop. Afghan dresses, jewellery, handicrafts, handmade carpets and paintings were on display. Late in the afternoon, I spoke to the painter who had been waving at me every time I went in and out of the coffee shop. Just before I met him I had read a report in the *Wall Street Journal* that the Taliban had now begun to force women to get married to its fighters in the conquered regions, which was tantamount to sexual violence of sorts.[6] The report also noted that in the captured places the Taliban had given directives that girls over fifteen and widows under forty had to be married off to their fighters. There were also tweets by the US embassy in Kabul saying the Islamist group was massacring Afghan soldiers, who were now surrendering to them in hordes. The US said such actions 'could constitute war crimes'.[7]

I sat with the painter, a man with a gentle smile, over a cup of chai subz to find out what had inspired him to become a painter, that too in a war zone like Afghanistan, which had hardly ever experienced peace. The painter, who was perhaps around forty, told me his father was a farmer, but he did not know if he was his real father because some of his cousins used to tease him saying he was his stepfather and that his real father had died fighting. He said the beauty of Afghanistan – its mountains, its deserts, its vastness – had inspired him to become a painter. His main source of inspiration was his father. He ran a small drawing school in one of the shanty corners of Kabul and taught both girls as well as boys in the age group of five to fifteen to draw and paint. While some wanted to draw pictures of mountains, lakes, rivers and birds, others wanted to draw portraits of American soldiers and the war, but the most popular subject for them was undoubtedly Shah Rukh Khan, particularly his 'dimpled smile', the painter said, his face blushing.

I knew what was coming, so before I could be asked I told him I had never met the Bollywood star, and he seemed pretty taken aback. We spoke for a long time about our lives, and then I asked him the inevitable what-if-the-Taliban-takes-over-Kabul question? His answer was also ready. He gave me a sharp look and said, directly looking into my eyes, 'I will die, they will kill me.' I told him what some experts had been saying – that this might be a new Taliban, a Taliban 2.0. He sighed and said nothing would be new in Afghanistan. Afghanistan would always remain the world's, America's, favourite battlefield, and so would the Taliban treat it, with the same attitude and fervour. His paintings were rather costly, and by the time we finished chatting he knew well that his paintings were not within my reach, but I wrote him a few lines of appreciation in his personal notebook, as I particularly fell for a painting that depicted the vastness of Mazar and its enormous mountains – all in hues of black, blue and brown. He told me he would always cherish those lines. We had even promised to stay in touch as we shared WhatsApp numbers. But since 15 August 2021 his number has been switched off. He had told me that even if he was killed his paintings would remain somewhere, continuing to depict Afghanistan as a land of beauty, a land of peace.

6

Has the Islamic Republic of Afghanistan Collapsed?

13 August 2021

'Ismail Khan captured!' All the Afghan news channels from TOLO to Ariana were flashing this on their screens even as Kabul continued to move on with its life unperturbed, almost like a bird in the sky focused only on flying and not concerned about what was happening on the land. Being a Friday, everyone was busy with their prayers and planning for the upcoming week. That's the beauty of Afghans. They behave as if the war is a sideshow which they tune into whenever they plan to do so; the rest of the time they are just getting on with their lives. I guess that's what war fatigue means.

As I sat down with my mandatory Americano at the Serena's beautifully curated garden, I wondered if I would at all be able to see the NATO forces withdrawing from Afghanistan, which was my original plan to cover. While growing up, I had seen images of Soviet forces withdrawing from Afghanistan in 1989, of tanks rolling out of the country like snails and ordinary Afghans waving at them. I was seven when my father showed me a

Reuters shot of a Soviet Union tank departing Shindand in Afghanistan in 1986 and local children waving at them, while a Russian soldier had a young boy on his lap giving him a farewell hug. Similar scenes were captured in other provinces such as Jalalabad and Termez – of smiling Soviet soldiers sitting atop tanks as they made their way out of that country slowly. A particular image that still haunts me is that of an Uzbek mother searching for her son among the soldiers. I guess that was the day I decided I would cover a development such as the one I was doing now.

The Soviet war in Afghanistan and the eventual withdrawal of the Russians from that country were somewhat along the pattern of what's happening between Russia and Ukraine at present. While this is not to say that Ukraine's situation is like that of Afghanistan during the Soviet invasion – and nobody with the slightest understanding of geopolitics can say that – there is nevertheless an uncanny similarity between the Soviet thinking and war strategy then and now.

The Soviets entered Kabul on 25 December 1979 with the primary aim of supporting the then pro-USSR communist regime in Afghanistan against the anti-communists of that time. Often referred to as the lasting legacy of the Cold War, the Soviet invasion of Afghanistan, which extended from 1979 to 1989, continues to create geopolitical disturbances globally, even to this day. This act of adventurism by the Russians was their last big move to defend international socialism and have another communist country in its neighbourhood before the USSR disintegrated in 1991. Moscow had been interfering in the internal politics of Afghanistan since 1978, in the aftermath of the Saur Revolution that took place in April 1978, out of which emerged the pro-communist and Soviet-backed People's Democratic Party of Afghanistan (PDPA) regime. The PDPA was successful in ousting the then president Mohammad Daoud Khan, who had ruled over Kabul from 1973 to 1978[1] after staging a coup against Afghanistan's last king Mohammad Zahir Shah. Afghanistan had been under a monarchical government since 1747. But Daoud's coup abolished monarchy from that country, and it was under him that Afghanistan entered a never-ending period of instability and chaos.

Some accounts say that this happened as a result of the KGB, Russia's former dreaded intelligence agency, actively supporting Nur M. Taraki, chief of the PDPA, catapulting him to the level of President, and his party comrades Hafizullah Amin to the post of prime minister and Babrak Karmal to the post of deputy prime minister. This meant an open invitation to the Soviets to come and make Afghanistan their playground. However, soon after assuming power, the PDPA got embroiled in internal factionalism, which at its foundation was a clash between communist ideology and Islamic beliefs, led by the Khalq and Parcham factions, respectively. There was much behind-the-curtains action, conducted by Russia's KGB, US's CIA and India's R&AW agents. Through all this, Soviet soldiers continued to plunder Afghanistan.[2]

HAS THE ISLAMIC REPUBLIC OF AFGHANISTAN   63

Eventually, the leaders of these conflicting factions either got killed, maimed or removed, paving the way for the entry of the Soviet-backed Mohammed Najibullah. It was under Najibullah's rule that the Taliban rose to become a force to be reckoned with in that country for the first time ever. Najibullah did have the support of the Soviets, but cracks were beginning to appear within the USSR and the Mujahideens were gaining strength. On 30 November 1987, the Loya Jirga adopted an Islamised constitution even as it elected Najibullah as the president of Afghanistan. The Loya Jirga is a grand council consisting of representatives from various ethnic and tribal communities with elders and popular local leaders as its members. It is convened during times of national emergency or crisis and has the right to select a new president. It is regarded as the highest forum representing the wishes of the Afghan people.

Najibullah changed the name of the country from the Democratic Republic of Afghanistan to the Republic of Afghanistan. He had come to power with the mandate to push forward a programme of national reconciliation by ending the conflict with the Mujahideens and broadening support for the government, which was the main objective of his launching the National Reconciliation Policy (NRP). Eventually, he started projecting himself as a great unifying leader of Afghanistan who was tolerant and modern in his thinking. But in reality, he faced disunity within his party and several coup attempts, and civil war raged in smaller pockets of the country with the withdrawal of troops by the Soviet Union.[3]

Coming back to my breakfast table at the Serena, I learnt that the capital of Helmand province, Lashkar Gah, and the capital of the western Badghis province, Qala-e-Naw, had also been captured. I kept wondering how long it would take for the Taliban to reach the borders of Kabul and how Kabul would defend itself. I visualised a bloody conflict between the Afghan government's forces and Taliban fighters on the streets of Kabul if that happened. I looked around and realised that some of the Americans with whom I used to chit-chat during breakfast were missing – even the man who told me before I left for Mazar that nothing would happen to Kabul. That day the breakfast area at the Serena was devoid of the usual chatter of people and clattering of plates. Some of my favourite waiters were also missing. Something was seriously wrong. Impatient as I was, I decided to venture out into some of the posh areas of Kabul and get a feel of what the people there were thinking. I called up some of my acquaintances who were teachers, scholars and artists. One of them called me over to a scrumptious homemade Afghan mantu (Afghan-style dim sum) lunch. Everyone I spoke to told me in an almost unanimous voice – 'The Taliban can never take over Kabul.' The elite will never talk real, I thought to myself.

I told my cab driver to take me to a beauty parlour and to a restaurant – establishments the Taliban detests – so I could find out what people there felt about the developments. I went to one of the famous beauty parlours in Kabul, owned and run by a bunch of proud

Afghan women who came from different ethnicities. Almost all of them had gotten their beautician certificates from Pakistan but had returned to Afghanistan because the American presence there gave them hope; and indeed the beauty industry in the country was booming. At the salon I did not straightaway jump into asking them questions as that might have made them feel uncomfortable. I wanted to first befriend them, so I opted for a beauty service. I was dumbfounded to see that they were doing a much better job than some of the most swish beauty parlours in Delhi. And it was cheap too! A beautician there, Gul, a fine, stylish woman in her late thirties, asked me on her own if I was from India – 'the land of Shah Rukh Khan and Deepika Padukone'. By then I was quite fed up with hearing the same question – whether I had met them – but I did not have the choice to speak my mind and simply nodded in agreement. She smiled and said she would give me another beauty service for free! That was a great offer, but I refused it. However, we started to speak, and the others joined in too.

My first question to this bunch of bright and promising women was, 'What if . . . What if the Taliban took over? What if all the beauty parlours were shut down, as they were back in 1996 when women were publicly flogged?' Two of them burst into laughter, and one of them said, 'Madam, this is not the Afghanistan of 1996. America has changed Afghanistan. The Taliban cannot do anything to us.' They even taunted me for creating fear in the hearts and minds of ordinary

Afghans. I asked Gul, who was their senior, what she thought of the current situation where province after province was collapsing under the galloping advance of the Taliban fighters and Kabul was swelling day by day with displaced persons and families. According to Gul, the Ghani government had the ability and power to check the advancing Taliban, and Afghanistan would see 'some kind of settlement'.

The story of Gul Jaan, as she was fondly called by her colleagues, was nothing short of a Bollywood script. After the Taliban came to power in 1996, Gul's parents left Afghanistan for Pakistan with their six children. The year was 1997, and Gul was three. They first settled in Lahore, where her father got a contractual job, and after a few years they settled in Islamabad, by which time Gul had passed high school and enrolled in a beautician's diploma course. She passed out from that school and immediately got a job in a modelling agency, and there was no looking back for her since. She claims to have groomed many Pakistani models and small-time actresses. However, after her marriage to an Afghan, who was also settled in Pakistan as a refugee, the couple decided to come back to their homeland and start their own family in Kabul. Today Gul has three children, she earns enough to provide a comfortable life to her family, and her husband works in a local hotel.

After I reached India, Gul and I spoke many times over WhatsApp. Her salon has been shut down permanently, and those young girls who believed in the

HAS THE ISLAMIC REPUBLIC OF AFGHANISTAN 67

Ghani government's ability to forge a peace settlement have fled to Iran. After the Taliban ordered the closure of schools for girls, Gul's daughters have been sitting at home learning household chores. The family is surviving only on her husband's meagre salary.

I wonder if in 2011, the tenth anniversary of the US's Afghanistan campaign, former US president Barack Obama, who ordered an additional 30,000 American troops to be posted there, thought about the millions of Afghan women like Gul. Apart from the US crackdown on Al-Qaeda, a key objective of the increased US presence was 'to reverse the Taliban's momentum and train Afghan security forces to defend their own country'.[4] If women like Gul felt the US had changed Afghanistan, were they wrong? After all, it was Obama who manifested to the world the 'audacity of hope' (Obama wrote a book, *The Audacity of Hope: Thoughts on Reclaiming the American Dream*, in 2006). When the Americans waged the war in Afghanistan they also brought hope to many innocent Afghans who had nothing to do with 9/11, nothing to do with America's War on Terror and nothing to do with Al-Qaeda. And then, with the Americans entering every corner of their cities and eventually their lives, Afghans thought they would be able to make Afghanistan a better country to live in, like it was before the Great Game. But nothing of the sort happened.

In fact, the Americans brought back the very Taliban they had ousted, shattering the hopes and dreams of millions of Afghans. Obama's announcement of the withdrawal of US troops was not welcomed as good news in Afghanistan. The gradual exit of American troops from Afghanistan from 2012 onward dealt a body blow to the Afghan forces, who were still undergoing training and were in a nascent stage.

Finally, I made my way to the temporary camps which housed the internally displaced people (IDP), as referred to in UN terminology. They had fled their homes and villages from the faraway Takhar and Kunduz provinces of rural and mountainous Afghanistan in search of a safer and better life in Kabul.

My visit to the camps was another story. I had teamed up with reporters from TOLO News, a leading TV channel headquartered in Kabul, hoping to get some assistance from them. While they were kind enough to hold the camera for me and also interpret what the locals told me there, I realised that they were there to do their own stories. Their editor was enraged that I had taken them to the Khair Khana camp in my taxi. When he came to know that they were with me, he sent for a bulletproof Land Cruiser SUV with two armed men to act as our bodyguards, a common practice followed by the Western media there. Some prominent Western media personnel even had former US Marine Corps as their bodyguards. Anyhow, I refused to take those benefits from TOLO, and while I was preparing to go to another camp that had come up in Shahr-e-Naw, one of their reporters asked me if I could get him an Indian visa. I promised to help, knowing well deep down that I could not. But somehow, in that moment, the helplessness in his eyes compelled me to make him that promise.

I asked him why he wanted to go to India when he had a well-paying job in one of Afghanistan's leading media organisations. He flatly told me, 'The Taliban is coming. And they will not spare us.' I froze. This was probably the first time since I had landed in Kabul that someone was telling me in absolutely clear terms that the Taliban was indeed coming. I was sitting in the bulletproof car as we waited for his other colleagues to come back, after which I would be setting off on my own. Two of his colleagues were busy working on their stories and I was already getting tense about how I would send mine to my office in Delhi. I wondered why, being a leading news channel, they had not covered the IDP story before even as refugees had been pouring into Kabul since June 2021. I asked him, 'Why do you think the Taliban will be able to take Kabul?' He said, 'Why do you not think they can take over Kabul? . . . The Americans have made a deal with them. They are now all-powerful. It is just a matter of days. All this talk of intra-Afghan talks [in Doha] by Abdullah and the withdrawal of troops by the end of the month is bullshit. We will all die. I love India and I want to pursue my higher studies there.'

I thought to myself . . . that's the quality of us journalists. We can see the future because we post-mortem the present and are able to see the reality for what it is as we have a more informed perspective than others. I wished him good luck and promised to help him. I left for the next campsite on my own. He believed I was 'fearless'. Little did he know that the sight of those children in the refugee camps made me feel miserable as a mother. I intensely missed my nine-year-old. I remembered the promise I made to him, which was to be back home before his birthday in August.

By the time I reached the campsite at Shahr-e-Naw it was late afternoon. I spoke to a few families there who were boarding buses to go somewhere. They were not ready to speak to me on camera and certainly not into the handheld mic. They feared the mic had 'hidden cameras' in it. I was quite taken aback by their thinking. I packed away all my gadgets in my bag and asked them why they thought that about my equipment. They said they thought I was an 'Indian agent'. I showed them my press identity card, and then they opened up. But it had to be off-camera. They said they were boarding those buses to go back to their villages from where they had come. They said the Afghan police had ordered them to return as the Taliban was coming to take over Kabul. They told me it was better to die in their own homes than to fight the Taliban in Kabul, which is not even their own place and a city where they were treated shabbily. They were angry and they were hungry. The government of the day did not provide them basic facilities like food, shelter and electricity in the camps where they lived. They were angry that despite sitting inside the filthy camps for months, no representative of the Ghani government had visited even once to ask about their condition.

An estimated 270,000 Afghans had been displaced inside the country between January and July 2021,

HAS THE ISLAMIC REPUBLIC OF AFGHANISTAN   71

primarily because of the insecurity and violence they were facing; and the total uprooted population stood at over 3.5 million, according to data released by United Nations High Commissioner for Refugees (UNHCR). In July that year, UNHCR spokesperson Babar Baloch warned of an 'imminent humanitarian crisis in Afghanistan . . . A failure to reach a peace agreement in Afghanistan and stem the current violence will lead to further displacement within the country, as well as to neighbouring countries and beyond'.[5]

This was the second time that I had heard the Taliban would indeed take over Kabul. Unfortunately, the global news media was awash with news of the Taliban facing a potential pushback as Ghani was preparing to fight them, and the Indian media was busy showing the so-called achievements of the Ghani regime. I wanted to write an article on this just a couple of days before the Taliban takeover of Kabul to say the capital would fall, but I was told by a senior editor in the organisation I worked for that the voices of a local reporter and a few villagers from rural Afghanistan did not make for a good story and that I should get 'more meat' to substantiate my claim that the Taliban was indeed winning and that the days of the Republic were numbered.

My plans to visit the gurdwara in Kabul did not fructify despite working hard for it, so I decided to try a famous restaurant located in the heart of the city known for its wide range of pizzas. It's called Bukhara Restaurant. I derive some sadistic pleasure in trying out pizzas in every country I visit, only to tell myself that India makes the worst pizzas in the world. Back in 2001, when I visited Pakistan on a college education trip, I tried a beef pizza in Islamabad, and its taste still lingers on my tongue. I ordered a beef pizza here too, with my cab driver for company. He was only too happy to eat at that restaurant, which was quite expensive by Afghan standards. A pizza had been a pipedream for him. He was appalled to see me biting into a beef pizza. He thought India was a land of vegetarians and nobody touched meat.

I came back to the hotel hoping to visit the gurdwara the next day as my request was still undergoing an approval process by the concerned authorities which ran the gurdwaras there. I knew for a fact that the Indian embassy would not help, so I tried to obtain permission using my local resources. However, I did speak to one of the officials at the embassy (name withheld, as he is still serving in the Indian Foreign Service) and described my experience of that day and also hoped that he would have some inkling as to what was happening on the ground. But once again I was told that everything was fine and they would want me to 'wrap up' fast from there and leave for India on the next available flight.

In that kaleidoscope of events I was in the midst of, I was quite surprised to see people from the most unexpected quarters, who had never bothered to have even a one-minute conversation with me in the past, flooding me with wishes on WhatsApp, Facebook and

LinkedIn. Pheww! Some were even lecturing me to 'not show off so much guts and come back to India'. Some sent me messages on a regular basis, but on my return went back to their old ways of throwing tantrums.

That evening I was contacted by both Suhail Shaheen, the Taliban leader based in Doha and now the organisation's international spokesperson, and the assistants of a former prime minister of Afghanistan, Gulbuddin Hekmatyar, popularly known as the 'Butcher of Kabul'.[6] I had been trying to connect with them for a very long time, much before I had even planned to visit Afghanistan. It was important for me to interview these people even as Afghanistan seemed to be going back in time. Shaheen had been extremely media-friendly ever since the Taliban had started to assume a more public profile. And Hekmatyar was that character who had once rattled the powers that be in Afghanistan.

I had written a short profile on Hekmatyar when he was contesting for the 2019 Afghan presidential elections. Ever since he secured an amnesty from the Ghani government in 2017, he had been planning to make a significant comeback in Afghanistan's politics. Once a ruthless anti-Soviet militia leader, Hekmatyar had said in one of his comeback speeches that he would seek to 'end the war and restore peace'.[7] He was given a warm reception by Ashraf Ghani. He had been forced to leave Afghanistan in 1996 when the Taliban came to power, and his party, the Hezb-e-Islami, is still fighting for its existence. I had studied so much about him and read many accounts of how he once ruled the roads of Kabul, and then about how he fell from grace, that I was extremely keen to meet him in person. A good friend of mine connected me with his party workers, who wanted to meet me before I could meet their chief. It seemed that my plan to interview Hekmatyar was finally coming true.

That evening I spent my time meeting a former Afghan diplomat who had once been posted in New Delhi and thereafter had been posted in the foreign ministry. He lived close to the Serena. We met over tea and chatted for many hours. He believed the Taliban was very close and that the Ghani government was losing the plot and was also being left high and dry by the Americans. 'The danger is lurking in the corners,' he said.

I asked him if it was different this time from the last time the Taliban had ruled Afghanistan. He told me, 'Last time it was only the Taliban and there was no concern about security in the country. Now there are factions of the Taliban and they don't work as one united force in Afghanistan.' He said there were now concerns about the existence and strengthening of some of the dreaded terrorist outfits like the Da'esh, East Turkestan Islamic Movement/Turkistan Islamic Party (ETIM), Lashkar-e-Taiba (LeT) and Jaish-e-Mohammed (JeM) because of the weak economy, lack of employment and income, and social evils. 'It's been a nightmare for everyone. They can kidnap anyone, kill anyone for a couple of thousand Afghani.'

Eventually, as the Taliban took over Kabul, dedicated government officials like him had to flee the country in a matter of moments, leaving behind everything as Taliban fighters were hunting out officials from the former Ghani government and killing them on the spot. My friend had two children, and although he and his wife were estranged, he took her along with him when he fled. After a lot of struggle he is now settled in London, but life is certainly not the same for him.

7

Mazar Gone; Can Kabul Be Far Behind?

14 August 2021

This was the day Mazar fell,[1] and it was now absolutely crystal clear to one and all that Kabul would be next! Just a few days earlier, Afghanistan's infamous Bagram Air Base and its prison with 5,000 inmates fell to the Taliban. The prisoners were all immediately recruited by the Taliban. It did not need rocket science for anyone to understand that Kabul was now in serious danger and that nothing and nobody was safe and nobody could or would save Kabul, least of all the international troops, who were fast packing their bags and heading back home leaving behind a chaotic, messy, poverty-stricken country!

Since the morning, speculation was rife in the Serena breakfast area that Ghani would be making a public address announcing a so-called peace deal or power-sharing pact with the Taliban. This was also what I had heard from the Indian embassy officials, who seemed to be more concerned about my presence there than about assessing the ground situation, which was changing every second. They once again asked me to leave, catching the first flight available. But I did not want to as I felt it was my responsibility towards my readers and my viewers to tell them what was happening on the ground. Just like the diplomats there, I was also doing my job.

This was the day I completed a week in Afghanistan, and I was bombarded with emails, messages and DMs thanking me for my reportage. People wanted more such reports because the other media organisations that had sent reporters to Afghanistan only showed the 'war' in its full glory, some by getting embedded with Afghan soldiers and some by making 'connections' with their sources. One reader said I was the 'only' journalist delivering hard-hitting and meaningful reports from Afghanistan. These encouraging words from those whom I had never met or seen gave me the inspiration to carry on with what I intended to do there.

Back at the Serena, I began to make plans to visit Kandahar. I thought Kandahar, after Mazar-i-Sharif, would be a good place to report from. But unlike Mazar, Kandahar looked immensely challenging since it had fallen to the Taliban a few days back, on 12 August. But I had one source who said he could help. I did not want to miss this opportunity for anything. But flights to Kandahar were thinning out by then, so I planned to travel by road. Thankfully, my cab driver agreed to take me. One of his aunts stayed in Kandahar, and we planned to stay the night there.

Kandahar was the birthplace of the Taliban and the place from where Mullah Omar had ruled at one time. Post the takeover by the Taliban in August 2021, while

Kabul remained the capital of Afghanistan, its ideological and spiritual capital was Kandahar. Also, once again the history student in me started to speak. After all, Kandahar was founded by Alexander the Great in 330 BC. Having come all the way to Afghanistan, I did not want to miss out on the opportunity to explore that city, which was steeped in history. Mullah Muhammad Omar had risen to power in 1996 when he proclaimed himself to be the leader of the Taliban in a grand ceremony at Kandahar's most revered shrine and got the title of Amir ul-Momineen – the highest religious title in Islam.

Just as I began to pack my bags, my mobile phone rang. It was Hekmatyar's men again, and this time they did not seem as serious as earlier and spoke with a smile in their voice. They informed me that Hekmatyar had agreed to give me an interview but I could not bring my own camera or mojo kit. The interview would be shot in his studio . . . Needless to say, I was shocked at the offer, because Hekmatyar was known to be very conservative. But I was happy, of course. Happy would be an understatement . . . I was thrilled.

Being a lone journalist in Afghanistan, I was relieved that I wouldn't have to bother with the lights, camera and mics and that my work would happen seamlessly. But they had one condition – his team wanted to take me out to dinner for an 'informal chat'. I agreed. I was ready to get this interview at any cost, and they seemed decent and polite enough to be trusted. They said they would pick me up from the Serena at 5 p.m. The venue would be disclosed later.

MAZAR GONE; CAN KABUL BE FAR BEHIND? 79

As soon as I finished with the conversation, I packed my bags and left for Kandahar, which was supposed to be a day's trip from Kabul. I hurried up as I had to return to Kabul by 5 p.m. Besides, it was impossible to stay back there anyway as the situation was fast turning grim. We crossed Kabul, which was comparatively more crowded than on other days, and straightaway hit the Kabul–Ghazni Highway/AH-1 and reached a place called Kala in a little more than an hour. News was now trickling in that Nangarhar had fallen as the Governor of the province had surrendered Jalalabad. So the Taliban had captured yet another semi-urban province without a fight.

This effectively meant that the Ghani government was now left with only Kabul. The capital of Afghanistan would be the next to fall. While nothing was yet confirmed, I dialled a few scholars and journalist friends who said panic had already taken over at Arg Palace, but they also spoke with surety about the president making a public address and some 'solution' being found. However, they were unanimous on one point – 'Come Back!' They asked me to come back to Kabul. If the capital city fell, they said, then all borders would be choked and I would be 'lost somewhere in the mountains, never to be found'. We reversed direction. My aborted Kandahar trip remains an incomplete chapter of my life, the unfulfilled dream of a reporter. Maybe someday it will come true.

On our way back I tried calling some of the senior Taliban leaders based in Doha to get an assessment of the situation and to find out what their plans were now; and most importantly, if there was really any 'solution' coming out of the talks that were going on there. I once again tried to connect with the press team of Dr Abdullah Abdullah and Dr Karzai, but they all seemed to have vanished into thin air. Something was amiss, I thought. Finally, I managed to speak to a Taliban leader (name withheld). It was a two- or three-minute WhatsApp call. He said, '*Madam, ab Kabul duur nahin*', with pride in his voice. I shuddered.

But still, I did not want to return to India. History was playing out in front of my eyes. How could I leave all that and come back . . . I felt guilty at the same time as my family, especially my son, were waiting for me back home. But I knew that one day he would understand, that one day he would draw courage from this, and that one day he would also learn what journalism is. He would know that his mother did not sit in a TV studio or in some editorial meeting dishing out meaningless, inauthentic stories or screaming at the top of her lungs to attract viewers and readers; she had been there in the midst of what was happening and had tried to bring back as many real stories as possible.

By the time I reached the Serena it was evening, and I waited for Ghani's address, like millions of others around the world. Just then, news came in that the Taliban had reached the gates of Kabul and were camping there, even as they vowed not to take power by force and would avoid bloodshed.

I started working the phones and spoke to an intelligence officer who was working under Mohib. A warm-hearted man, he was always eager to help me. He was now more worried about his own life and wanted to escape. He had booked tickets for himself and his family for 15 August to fly out of the country. So this was like his 'last conversation' with me, as he did not know at the time where fate would be taking him.

He said there was absolute panic in the presidential palace and that Ghani was on his way out. 'How can he?' I asked; the President was about to address the nation. He said the video address had been pre-recorded the previous evening, i.e., on 13 August. He said that as a last-ditch effort, Mohib had spoken to all the service chiefs to make a final assessment of the situation even as Kabul was completely surrounded. I felt numb.

Mohib, he said, was concerned because the President had recorded the previous evening that Afghan forces, with support from the government, would continue to fight the Taliban. The NSA thought otherwise, because the murmurs in the war cabinet were that the forces had all given up as resources and support had dried up. Reports of Dostum and Noor leaving the country rattled the very core of the government as they were the last ones standing up to the Taliban, albeit in a very weak manner. But their presence, nevertheless, had been a psychological boost to the Afghans. They had now escaped to various countries, mainly in Central Asia, while their men were roaming around Afghanistan incognito. While some had escaped, some got killed at the hands of the Taliban.

Some of Ata Noor's closest aides, who are still in contact with me, kept waiting at the Dustlik (Friendship) Bridge, for two or three days after the takeover, only to be pushed back into the country again as the gates of the bridge at the entry point to Uzbekistan were not allowed to be opened for them. One of them had his family living in India, so he sought the Indian government's help to come to India as their visas had been revoked, and reapplying for the visas would mean getting exposed to the Taliban. The Dustlik (Friendship) Bridge was built in 1982 connecting Afghanistan with Uzbekistan for the supply of Soviet troops to Afghanistan. It also has a rail link. The railway link was later expanded to reach Mazar-i-Sharif in 2011.

Interestingly, while the Embassy of Uzbekistan remained fully functional in Kabul post the return of the Taliban, the Tashkent government temporarily shut down the entire 144-kilometre border it shares with Afghanistan, even while it carried out business as usual with the new interim government in Kabul. Meanwhile, as Ata Noor left with his sons for that country, he spoke about a 'conspiracy' that had led to the return of the Taliban.

The former governor of Balkh wrote in a letter:

Dear and esteemed countrymen! Unfortunately, the depth of the conspiracy, as a result of which Balkh collapsed, is very deep. The conspiracy is now facing Kabul and its leaders. Despite our firm resistance, sadly, all the government and the ANDSF equipment were handed over to the Taliban as a result of a big organised & cowardly plot. They had orchestrated the plot to

MAZAR GONE; CAN KABUL BE FAR BEHIND?

trap Marshal Dostum and myself too, but they didn't succeed . . . Our path won't end here.

The ex-governor also blamed the US for leaving Afghanistan 'irresponsibly', which too had exacerbated the problems and led to the return of the Taliban. He wrote:

> So, after 20 years, our expectation was that they would, at least, before withdrawal, make sure that there is stability in this region, there is development in this country and rights of the people are guaranteed. However, they did not wait for that, they did not see that but in fact they withdrew irresponsibly.[2]

Back in the war cabinet, Afghan Defence Minister Bismillah Khan Mohammadi informed Mohib that mounting a resistance at Panjshir Valley also looked 'impossible' as his forces had 'stopped fighting completely'. Panjshir Valley has, historically, always stood up against the Taliban, whether during the 1980s, the 1990s or the early 2000s.

Mohib and others in Ghani's close ring of ministers, including the then vice president Amrullah Saleh, were believed to have had a heated debate on whether or not to run the recorded video message by Ghani. According to another source of mine who was in the know of the situation, while Ghani and his men were scrambling to defend Kabul as the Taliban was closing in rapidly, their newly appointed Chief of Army Staff Haibatullah Alizai had chalked out a two-pronged plan to defend Kabul as

84   THE FALL OF KABUL

well as to fight the Taliban with the creation of a 'special force' of sorts. This would include soldiers not only from the Afghan Army, which was fast depleting by then, but also young men from the Afghan counterterrorism units, also known as 'Zero Units', which had been closely working with the American and Afghan intelligence agencies. Ali had sought three days to a week to carry out the operation of flushing out the Taliban from the country.[3]

While both Ghani and Mohib were impressed with his plan, it ultimately failed to fructify. As the hours went by, panic heightened and everything seemed to collapse as the Taliban announced that it had captured Mazar late that night.

However, after a lot of haggling among his team, Ghani's pre-recorded message was finally aired. In the speech he said, probably banking on Alizai, that he would work towards remobilising the Afghan national security forces, which he said was his 'top priority'. He said he would not allow the Taliban to carry on with the 'imposed war'. He also promised to find ways to help the thousands of people displaced by the fighting across the country.[4]

While all this was playing out, I was sitting a few kilometres away, at an open-air Turkish joint with Hekmatyar's men. They had wanted to meet me informally before I interviewed their chief. They wanted to discuss with me the questions I wanted to ask Hekmatyar, as it was rare for him to give interviews to Indian journalists. The cafe was mostly filled with

MAZAR GONE; CAN KABUL BE FAR BEHIND? 85

men pulling at hookahs and eating kebabs served on storeyed platters. There were men of all shapes and sizes, and they were all talking loudly. I was probably the only woman in the cafe that night, but nobody made me feel uncomfortable or uneasy. But so I would not attract any undue attention, and since it was an open-air place, I sat with my head covered. The environment was more casual and easy-going than at a Starbucks cafe in central Delhi – where, by the way, I do not feel at ease at all.

Nevertheless, the air inside the cafe was thick with speculation. Everyone was discussing Ghani's address and Mazar's fall at the same time. At that moment and in the middle of all that panic and chaos and confusion, it did not occur to anyone that Ghani's was a pre-recorded message. Somehow, everyone latched on to every single word he spoke that night, including me. I guess that was the real 'fog of greater or lesser uncertainty' that Carl von Clausewitz, the famous military thinker, spoke about when he described war in his book *On War*.

We finished the dinner with Turkish coffee, and as they had picked me up from the hotel, they dropped me back too. As we were reaching the Serena, one of them asked me how he could visit India. I asked him why he wanted to. He said he had studied medicine in Chennai and 'misses Indian food'. He asked me if he could seek medical treatment in India by faking an ailment. I discouraged him. Just as I was about to get out of the car, he told me, 'We are not safe here, anything can happen to any one of us. They [the Taliban] are right outside Kabul.' It was 10.30 p.m. I said goodbye to them, promising to meet them the next morning.

Kabul seemed uncomfortably busy that night. The roads from Shahr-e-Naw, where the cafe was located, to my hotel took longer than usual. Even at night, while I sat beside the window of my room in the Serena, sipping coffee, I saw American bombers and C-17s fly overhead, one after the other. That afternoon I had even seen smoke billowing out of the US embassy building from the Serena rooftop; they were burning all their sensitive documents before evacuating the place. Eventually, we would leave this country, I thought to myself, but what about the Afghans we will leave behind? What about that mother in the refugee camp who looked at me helplessly? What about that girl I met at Mazar airport who came to Kabul with me on the same flight hoping to make it to India someday for a better future?

I closed yet another night sitting in bed and dozing off with one of Ahmed Rashid's books in hand. I don't know when I fell asleep. Next day was the big day, when I was about to do something that no other journalist in India could pull off – interview the 'Butcher of Kabul'.

8

Taliban Back in Kabul, and I Stranded on the Streets

15 August 2021

Karl Marx had said, 'History repeats itself, first as tragedy, second as farce.' Growing up I often heard my mother quote this line and I would ask her what it meant, and every time I asked she would explain it patiently to me. But the real meaning of this line played itself out right in front of my eyes on 15 August 2021 – the day the Taliban came back to power while the world watched in shameful silence.

The day began normally, although I was slightly tense as I had an interview scheduled with Hekmatyar. I was told that he was extremely particular about everyone being on time and was himself always a punctual man. I skipped breakfast that morning but still went down to the restaurant to have my coffee for my daily dose of energy. The usually buzzing cafe at the Serena was eerily devoid of its usual patrons. By now even the staff had thinned out significantly. When I asked the duty manager about the absence of some of the waiters with whom I had developed an affinity and from whom I would get information on what's happening around, I was told they were on leave.

In between sipping my coffee and prepping for the Hekmatyar interview, I watched the news. A chill ran down my spine, and for a couple of minutes I felt absolutely frozen. I wondered if all was gone. The television anchor was saying that tension was building up on the Kabul–Jalalabad highway and that it would take only a 'few hours' for the Taliban to reach the eastern gates of Kabul. Suddenly I saw a cameraman from Al Jazeera rushing towards the terrace of the Serena. Serena's terrace was famous for its bird's eye view of Kabul city. I followed him and saw the entire gaggle of international reporters on the terrace reporting live from there. The message was clear – the Taliban was knocking at the doors of Kabul.

I guess this is why they say ignorance is bliss. Had I not been making ambitious plans, unaware, even up to the very moment of hearing this news, that the Taliban was inside Kabul, I would not be able to move an inch out of the hotel now, forget about carrying on with my work. But my thoughts turned to my interview. I was soon going to be part of that minority of global reporters who had interviewed Hekmatyar. And nothing at the moment had the capacity to stop me from doing that interview.

Just as I was leaving for my room, I again heard the news that Ghani's aide at the presidential palace, Salam Rahimi, was still deeply engaged in clinching a last-minute deal with the Taliban fighters, who were all waiting at the gates of Kabul. They were reportedly promising not to attack the capital and 'take power by

TALIBAN BACK IN KABUL

force'; they were waiting for a 'favourable peace deal' to be arrived at. Rahimi got the Taliban to cough up a deal that all foreigners would be given safe passage to exit the country and nobody would be harmed. But Ghani was not convinced and he wanted to launch an attack.

Something in me said this was all a farce. If they couldn't clinch a deal for so long, what was going to change in the next few hours? It was just a matter of time before the Taliban walked right into Kabul. I asked my favourite waiter at the Serena coffee shop, who always served the right coffee to everyone, what was happening. In his halting English, with a bit of Pashto and Hindi, he told me, 'Madam, Taliban is already here, what is this thing that everyone says Taliban at the gate, Taliban will enter Kabul, Blah! Blah! The people whom they are stopping at the gates are the fighters, who do not understand these games such as peace deals, they only understand blood and their only motto in life is to kill . . . They are right now exhausted and following orders from Doha, where their leaders are actually doing the deal. These are useless fellows. And let me tell you the Taliban is already inside this city. They are within us. All they need is a trigger and they will attack from within.'

I asked him what he would do if they came in. He said, 'I do not fear them. I only worry if they will shut down this hotel and take away my job. Other than that I don't fear them. The corrupt men of Ghani should start running now.'

Just as I reached my room to get ready and leave for Hekmatyar's residence-cum-office, I received a call from one of my sources. He was shouting at the other end, asking me to 'leave immediately' or 'face the ugly consequences'. I told him to calm down and asked him what had happened. He said Vice President Amrullah Saleh had already left the capital for Panjshir Valley, apparently with a plan to mount a resistance against the Taliban. But Ghani, Mohib and the others, though still contemplating whether to mobilise troops to attack the Taliban or not, were also making preparations to escape from Afghanistan.

Deep in his mind, Ghani was probably clear about one thing – he would not meet the same end as the former communist president Najibullah,[1] who was dragged by the Taliban from a hideout inside the UN premises and killed. His body was hung from a lamppost to instil fear in the minds of the people.

A Pashtun, young, charming and energetic, Najibullah was successful in convincing the Russians during the Soviet occupation that he was fit to be the leader of Afghanistan and only he could unite all the ethnic tribes of that country. Under the guidance of the Soviets, Najibullah was elected on 4 May 1986. By 1990 he had positioned himself as a 'confident unifying force',[2] even as his opponents continued their infighting, hungry to come to power. The Afghans seemed content under his rule and Afghan society got some semblance of stability as he was able to maintain a steady supply of food and also somewhat secured the country from its adversaries.

War fatigue and the failure of his opponents to put up a united front against him made Najibullah's position stronger and firmer. This was seen as the single biggest reason why the Soviets continued to favour Najibullah even after they left the country. But what gradually became apparent was that Najibullah was beginning to get worried, and he began to confide in his close aides. His regime was slowly coming under threat from multiple factors, such as disunity within his own party, repeated coup attempts and militant resistance, which kept the country on tenterhooks even as a civil war-like situation simmered.

As Kabul fell to the Mujahideen and unrest swelled across Afghanistan by the summer of 1992, Najibullah – the last communist leader of Afghanistan – found refuge in the UN compound in Kabul, where he lived from 1992 to 1996, translating Peter Hopkirk's *The Great Game* from English to Pashto. He had told one of his visitors who came to meet him at the UN campus, 'Afghans keep making the same mistake.'[3]

Finally, on that fateful day of 27 September 1996, Taliban fighters gatecrashed into the UN premises and pulled Najibullah out. They beat him up and tied him to their truck and dragged him through the streets of Kabul as they drove the vehicle around. Finally, they castrated him before hanging his dead body from a lamppost with US dollar bills stuffed in his mouth. His brother was also hanged with him at the main traffic circle of Kabul.[4]

Ghani could not be blamed if he harboured fears of meeting Najibullah's fate; however, he left the country in abject poverty while he lives a lavish life in another country. And as the Taliban came back to power, this time too the fundamentalist group was punishing many, allegedly kidnapping, killing them and hanging their bodies from cranes in the province of Herat. Mullah Nooruddin Turabi, a dreaded Taliban leader, had said in a media interview that year that the Taliban would carry out public executions, as it used to earlier.[5]

'Everyone criticised us for the punishments in the stadium, but we have never said anything about their laws and their punishments . . . No one will tell us what our laws should be. We will follow Islam and we will make our laws on the Quran . . . Cutting off of hands is very necessary for security,' Turabi had said in an interview with the Associated Press.[6]

During its last rule, the Taliban was criticised severely by the Western media for carrying out public executions inside stadiums and crowded places. Turabi was referring to that and was saying that the West would not dictate to them when it came to their following and implementing Islamic laws. By 'their laws and their punishments' he meant Western/ American laws and punishment methods.

To come back to my Sunday at the Serena, I quickly got ready and left for Hekmatyar's interview. I was already running late as my cab arrived late that morning. The driver told me he had witnessed unusual traffic jams on the roads. That was my second signal for the day.

Ignoring every scenario that screamed 'danger' at me, I left for Hekmatyar's interview, which was scheduled for 10.30 a.m. at the Daftar-e-Markazi (the main office of Hezb-e-Islami party) on Darulaman Road, near the

American University. When I asked my cab driver how far it was from the Serena, and he said twenty minutes. The distance was huge, considering it was Kabul. But to me it came as a relief as it gave me more time to review the questions I had planned to ask the former prime minister of Afghanistan.

Like every day, Kabul was crowded, but unlike every day, Kabul looked erratic. The crowd — men, women and children — had no pattern to the way it moved. The movement at the shops too looked haphazard, and there was worry and tension on the faces of each and every person on the road. People were walking on the roads in large groups; families walking with big bags and sacks on their shoulders, and each and every car was full of people — something I hadn't seen the whole week I had been there. I asked my cab driver, who came from the same local transport agency as the previous one, if he thought the Taliban would take over Kabul. I always believed in gathering local intelligence. He scoffed at the idea, saying I was being a 'typical foreign journalist' who sees ghosts where there are none. He told me he was a Hazara and that his entire family was doing well in Kabul; they knew for a fact that the Americans were not going to let the Taliban enter Kabul.

Unlike the previous cab driver, this one was a bit hesitant to talk. It seemed to me that he also did not like it that he was on duty driving around a non-white, non-Western journalist — someone who could not be tapped for obtaining visas or dollars should he have to flee. He was one of those Afghans who did not think India was an option for him for relocation.

We reached Hekmatyar's office before time. As expected, it was heavily guarded and there was a sense of being watched as you moved inside the sprawling campus. But I wasn't subjected to any kind of checking as I met one of his senior party officials at the entry gate itself. He was returning from a nearby fruit shop. He seemed relaxed for the day. The Sunday mood had seeped deep into Afghan society, I guess owing to the Americans.

He guided me through the maze of the garden and got my car parked near a three-storeyed building where the interview was to take place. I was ushered in by another senior party worker into the main room, which was done up like a proper TV studio, with two or three cameras and lights. I was told Hekmatyar would arrive on time. I went through my questions one more time, and it then occurred to me that he would be speaking in Pashto, and as with my interview with Ata Noor, I would need someone to translate for me as he spoke.

Thankfully, I was carrying two mobile phones as part of my ubiquitous mojo kit, which helped me in audio-recording the interview. Since the interview was to be shot by them, I used my mojo kit for other useful purposes. Thankfully I had carried it with me, which helped me report the interview because they had real trouble in sending me the video as they had to run for safety immediately after the interview was over as Kabul had fallen by then.

Coming back to the interview, as I was getting anxious about the translation part, I was introduced to someone who volunteered to translate the entire interview. He looked sharp and had an American accent. I realised only after returning to the hotel later that day that he was none other than Hekmatyar's grandson Obaidullah Baheer, a journalist and lecturer at the American University of Afghanistan. Within minutes, Hekmatyar entered the room and there was absolute silence. I was quite nervous inwardly, but he made me feel at ease immediately. He was dressed in his usual attire, in a uniquely styled black turban and jacket. His gentle and polite demeanour somehow gave me the confidence to carry on with my work.

It was not easy for me to interview important figures in Afghanistan, most of whom would promise to speak to me but either refuse later or simply turn me down, seeing that I was from India and did not have deep pockets, unlike the Western journalists. Some had also questioned my integrity and work experience.

I gave Baheer my old phone so he could speak into it, translating his grandfather's answers for me, which he did diligently. But he did not have to translate my questions, posed in English, to Hekmatyar, who was well versed in the language. Between six and eight of Hekmatyar's men entered the room and the camera and lights were switched on. I thought, 'This is it' – the moment I had been waiting for for such a long time.

I began, 'You've been Afghanistan's prime minister, then you fought the 2019 elections hoping to become the President. But today it seems history has come a full circle in Afghanistan . . . Your thoughts?'

Hekmatyar replied, 'The US never invested in or supported the popular figures [who fought the Taliban locally]. The US made a mistake within Afghanistan in that they invested in people who were not popular locally. The major reason behind the collapse of the government, the defeat of the NATO allies is investment in unpopular figures [like Ghani]. Their [NATO] coming to Afghanistan was a blunder and then the way they went out was a blunder, and now we have seen them [Taliban] come back again, which just goes to prove the point that their withdrawal was a mistake to begin with.'[7]

According to Hekmatyar, it was inevitable that the Taliban would grow more powerful. He said the 'only way forward would be to hold elections', wherein an 'impartial transitional government' should be formed. Hekmatyar, who had contested the 2019 presidential election, called it 'sham' and 'fraudulent'. In that election, Ashraf Ghani had been elected the President of Afghanistan.[8]

He said the very fact that the Taliban was able to take over province after province with such immense speed showed the failure of the Ghani administration. And all this while the insurgents were marching into the Afghan capital.

Sitting inside that office, none of us was aware of what was going on at that very moment outside the walls of the Daftar-e-Markazi itself.

Just as the interaction was going deeper and the stiff atmosphere in the room was easing a bit, I realised that some commotion was taking place behind the camera and everyone was murmuring in tense voices. I was signalled to stop the interview and close it ASAP! Sensing the tension, I did exactly that.

However, many of my questions remained unanswered. I was keen to ask Hekmatyar about his long periods of interaction with a former CIA chief – Milt Bearden – who had manned the agency's Islamabad station in 1987. Bearden cultured Hekmatyar to a great extent, giving him hundreds of millions of US dollars in aid, which came out of the pockets of American taxpayers. And yet Hekmatyar had refused to visit New York to meet the 'infidel' Ronald Reagan, the US President at the time. Bearden and his team eventually came under scrutiny for supporting Hekmatyar and other Afghan leaders who were working in close collaboration with Pakistan's ISI. During one of their interactions, Hekmatyar, who spoke excellent English, had told Bearden that he knew the CIA was planning to kill him. Bearden asked him, 'Why would I want to kill you?' Hekmatyar said, 'The US can no longer feel safe with me alive.' Later, Bearden, when asked about this statement by Hekmatyar in an interview, said, 'I think the engineer flatters himself.'[9]

Hekmatyar, an engineer by qualification, served as Afghanistan's prime minister for two brief terms before the Taliban takeover in 1996. In 1975, he founded the Hezb-e-Islami Party, considered to be one of Afghanistan's powerful jihadi groups, to fight the

Soviets, and that was why he was the CIA's favourite. Later, his group split and he renamed his faction Hezbe-Islami Gulbuddin (HIG). Post 9/11, Hekmatyar declared jihad against the US and began his support of the Taliban. In February 2003, the US listed him as a 'Specially Designated Terrorist' and his HIG as a 'Group of Concern.'

As I stepped outside his office – almost being shunted out while Hekmatyar, surrounded by his aides, vanished into thin air – I found my cab driver on the verge of leaving the campus. He looked as if someone had stabbed him in the back. I asked him what had happened as I jumped into the car, and he said, 'The Taliban is on the road, I have to reach home. I was about to leave this place.' I was shocked to hear that, but I understood his concerns too. I asked him to take the shortest route possible to the Serena. But he was in no mood to take orders or listen to me; he did not even seem to care that I was in the car.

The moment we left Hekmatyar's office, he accelerated and drove at a speed of 120 kmph on a road where the right bay was clogged with cars and the left had been kept free by the police for movement of vehicles as the police had planned to chase and hunt down the Taliban. I asked him to slow down or there might be an accident. He told me, 'It's better to die in an accident than at the hands of the Taliban.' And that was the very last time he spoke to me on that journey. He refused to even acknowledge that I was in the car. He touched 125 kmph, and just as we reached Maywand Cinema, which was 3.5 kilometres from the Serena, smoke began to billow out of the car, which came to a complete stop.

We were stuck in the middle of a busy marketplace where there was a huge traffic jam. People were running in all directions toting locally made rifles, some even AK-47s, and they were screaming at us as our car had blocked the entire road. There were some dingy shops lining the road, selling anything from beef burgers to boiled eggs and hardware products. I made an attempt to come out of the car, but my driver shouted and said if I got out I might get killed. Onlookers began to peep in at my window as I clearly looked like an outsider.

The driver opened the bonnet of the car, and immediately a gush of smoke engulfed the vehicle and the surroundings. Just as the smoke began to thin out I found that he was gone. I did not know what to do. I called one of my editors, but the phone went unanswered. It was a Sunday after all. I frantically began to call my husband, who calmed me down and asked me to do whatever it would take to reach the Serena. People were slowly surrounding the car – only to have a look at me, it seemed at that moment. Angry and curious looks filled the windows of my cab. I grabbed my belongings and jumped out of the car. I spotted my driver speaking to three or four men; they seemed to be chatting about the car. Seeing me they came running and asked me to stand on the pavement, which was littered with garbage. I stood there and asked the driver to call the hotel to send for another car. He refused. I then began calling the hotel myself but realised my prepaid amount for my cell phone service had run out. I called the hotel again, using my international roaming facility. I was informed that the hotel had been shut down temporarily as the Taliban had taken over the city and Ghani and his team had left the country. The man at the hotel reception spoke like a TV news anchor and hung up. I stood there like a stone in the midst of that immense commotion. Only then did it dawn on me that these people who were holding guns were locals who wanted to confront and kill the Taliban, who had now spread around the entire city.

I looked at my driver helplessly, hoping for some help from him. But for him my chapter was over for that day. He was busy with the local car mechanics he had managed to bring over. The mechanics flung open the backseat where I had been sitting in order to get the toolkit out to fix the car. I prodded the driver again to call one of his colleagues who offered cab services to the Serena. He tried calling the same driver with whom I had pizza the other day. Fortunately, he was at the hotel with this car but he was not able to come and pick me up as the hotel was locked. My driver said he would have to focus on getting his car fixed. He also did not want me to stand there talking loudly into the phone as I was apparently inviting trouble. By then almost an hour and a few minutes had passed since the car had broken down. My husband started calling me frantically, but my phone battery was dying and I did not know what to tell him.

Realising that my driver would not help, I started to walk towards the hotel. One of the mechanics was kind enough to show me the exact route to the hotel. I had become a little familiar with the route to the hotel, but this was a shortcut I was shown and soon I felt slightly lost, though I kept to the route I was told to take. I had walked perhaps 300 metres when I was joined by a group of five or six men who started to query me. I did not want to avoid them and walk away because each had a gun hanging from his shoulder. I answered none of their questions but just said 'India' and 'Hindi'. Their angry expressions immediately changed into a kind of fanboy look, and one of them said, 'Shah Rukh Khan', pointing his finger at me as if to indicate that I was that superstar. I said yes in Hindi. And they were so elated that they agreed to 'escort' me up to the Serena. One of them told me in proper Hindi that the Taliban was everywhere and if they saw me, a woman from a different community walking alone, they would immediately abduct or shoot me. Everything at that moment seemed too surreal. I could not figure out if this was truly happening to me or if I was just having a nightmare.

After walking a few metres with me, one of them asked me what was I doing on the road. I told them the reason, and they seemed quite taken aback. They were looking at me questioningly, as if to ask why I had gone to interview Hekmatyar. And then in minutes they left me and walked into an alley because they learnt that some Taliban fighters had entered the residential complexes and were killing people. I had no choice but to keep walking. I was about 100 metres from the hotel when I saw the other driver draw up beside me in his car, honking. I still do not know how he found me. I got into the car, and on the way saw small groups of Taliban men zipping through the city in their pickup trucks, and that was when the reality of my situation fully sank in. I could make out that they were the Taliban as they had their signature white flag (the *Shahada*, or the Taliban flag, is currently the unofficial flag of Afghanistan) stuck on their bonnets.

At the Serena, the security guards refused to let me in. They let me in when I showed them my room keys, but not before giving me a ticking off, asking me why I had been out of the hotel early that morning. By then I had also lost my sanity and yelled back, saying I too was working just as they were. They smiled in a condescending manner, which only a woman can recognise, and I was allowed to pass the first of the three gates. It felt like I was home.

I entered the reception area and found it to be absolutely empty except for one of the front office managers. I rushed to my room, which was at the far end of the second floor. Walking through the decorated corridors to my room, I became aware of the eerie silence in and around the hotel that day. I entered my room and sat on the bed for seven minutes straight and broke down in tears. Suddenly, I got a call from Shekhar Gupta, who consoled me and asked what had happened. I explained the situation to him. After the call I realised it was almost 1 p.m. and that I hadn't eaten a grain of food. I called the reception to check if the hotel kitchen was functioning, and they urged me not to step out of the room as the Taliban could enter the hotel any moment. Some of their local leaders were already trickling in.

I switched on the TV and saw that the news cycle had completely changed from what had been showing early morning when I was leaving for the Hekmatyar interview. I was shocked to learn that Ghani, Mohib, Atmar and others had all left the country, leaving the Afghans in the hands of the Taliban. Within a few minutes I saw the capital of a country entirely collapse, like a sand edifice. It hit me fully right at that moment – the Taliban was indeed back.

I settled in my small study in the hotel room, which at that moment was the safest refuge in my entire world, and started writing out a report on what I had seen on the streets. By the latter half of the day, calls and messages started pouring in from India asking me to come back and be safe. Some of them were kind and compassionate while some sounded more like commands. I particularly remember calling up one of our former foreign secretaries a few days after my return to India to get his comments for an unrelated story, and the first word he used for me was 'foolhardy'. He thought it was 'stupid' of me to go to Afghanistan to report.

Well, back to Serena Hotel. After filing my report, I planned to check on the other journalists living in the hotel. I spoke to them over the intercom and met a few at the coffee shop. There I was told that the Taliban had surrounded the hotel and would soon be undertaking a door-to-door search of the entire hotel to see if any official of the Ghani administration was hiding there. I was petrified as I was alone. For a second I wondered if the Taliban, during the so-called search operation, would shoot me. I began calling up my sources again to get a sense of what exactly had happened while I was shut out from the world. This time it wasn't easy and I was unable to contact anyone, as most of them were busy packing their bags to leave Afghanistan. After trying the entire afternoon, I finally got through to one of my Afghan journalist friends, who too was planning to leave the country, but not immediately. He asked me to meet him outside AZIZI Bank, which was almost 3 kilometres from the Serena. At first I refused, because even if it was nearby it was extremely risky at that time to move out as the Taliban was fast spreading across the city.

Thankfully, the Serena lifted its lockdown by that time. Gathering whatever courage I had left in me, I left for AZIZI Bank. My journalist friend picked me up from the Serena and I did not think even once before sneaking out of the hotel in his car. I always believed one thing about journalism – anything that is structured is not meant for it. Thanks to my friend's efficient driving, we reached AZIZI Bank without any trouble. I did notice that some of the police posts that had been there even that morning were gone. After reaching the bank, we met one of our common friends, a women's rights activist, and she gave me some 'inside-the-palace scoop'.

I could not write about those accounts as everything moved too fast thereon. Much against my wishes, my office asked me to leave Afghanistan the next day. They

A vegetable seller passes through Mazar-i-Sharif's main square. After the Taliban captured the city, portraits of former president Ashraf Ghani were torn down and the tricolour flag was replaced with the Shahada banner of the Islamic Emirate of Afghanistan.

Children sell boiled eggs, Afghan naan, water bottles and fruit at a main traffic intersection in Kabul.

A busy intersection, the Great Massoud Circle in Kabul is close to the US embassy and a US military base. In 2014, a bomb blasted by the Taliban killed three NATO soldiers. On 15 August 2022, the Taliban held a major congregation at the circle to mark their victory and signal the defeat of resistance forces.

Author interviewing Gulbuddin Hekmatyar, former prime minister of Afghanistan, on 15 August 2021.

A library inside the Blue Mosque with a rare collection of texts dating back to the 13th century. Islamic scholars from around the world visit the library for higher studies and research.

Former governor of Balkh Province Ata Mohammad Noor at his office-cum-residence in Mazar-i-Sharif before it fell.

The main tarmac of Mazar-i-Sharif airport where people were queuing up to board a Kam Air flight headed to Kabul long past midnight. This was two days before Mazar fell.

Author holding a bullet shell while waiting for her flight back to India at the Kabul airport. The suitcase in the photograph was taken away at the Indian embassy during evacuation and never returned.

TALIBAN BACK IN KABUL

had booked me on the first Air India flight out of Kabul the following day. But on the ground I knew the situation was going from bad to worse, and I had doubts that commercial flights would be operating. Besides, I wanted to stay back and report for another week or so. History was unravelling right before my eyes and I did not want to miss those moments for anything. But, as fate would have it, I was booked on a flight that never took off as the aircraft that was to fly in from India did not arrive in the first place.

So my activist friend and I wandered over to AZIZI Bank. She had to take out money from the ATM as rumours were flying thick that the Taliban would seize the operations of all banks. We were standing at the end of the snaking queue to the ATM, when suddenly my friend broke down. She said one of her brothers, who was a soldier in the Afghan Army, had been killed while fighting the Taliban a few days back and the family had come to know only now. My journalist friend told me he had heard that there was a commotion going on in the palace as the Taliban fighters had breached the understanding reached with the Ghani government that it would not take power by force after its capture of Maidan Shahr, capital of the central Afghan province of Wardak, 40 kilometres west of Kabul. The Taliban fighters, apparently, entered Kabul from that area even as their bosses sitting in Doha were clueless about it. I had heard from another source that the Doha bosses had given strict orders to the fighters to not enter Kabul in haste, and when they did they were asked to 'retreat and wait for further orders'.

The Taliban also issued a statement to say it did not intend to enter Kabul by force or by waging war but would negotiate with the other side to enter peacefully. By then Ghani had fled, and that news spread like wildfire. So the Taliban found it easy to take charge as the previous government served the nation on a platter to them. Chaos and resentment, anger and fear, and a complete sense of helplessness gripped the entire capital city. Adding to the confusion was yet another former president of Afghanistan, Hamid Karzai, who did not want to lose out on this opportune moment and immediately tweeted that he was creating a coordination council comprising Abdullah, who theoretically retained the fancy title of the chairman of the High Council for National Reconciliation, and Hekmatyar.[10] As time proved, every decorated promise fell flat as the Taliban gradually gained control of the country, taking it back to the dark ages.

I asked my friend what her plans were. She said she would stay back in Kabul and continue with her activism. 'This is the time. How can I just pack my bags and leave? My country needs me. I will fight the Taliban by staying back in this country,' she said. She seemed fairly sure that Taliban 2.0 would not be any different from Taliban 1.0 and would restrict education for girls, shut down schools and universities and also stop women from working. 'It will be all the same and I cannot sit silently now.' I thought she was overthinking and that this Taliban would not take any such regressive steps since it had to fight for legitimacy. We finally decided to part ways. She could not withdraw the amount she wanted as the ATMs began to run out of money and a limit was imposed on how much could be withdrawn. My journalist friend gave me a look that said 'we may never meet again'. His brother's family lived somewhere in Germany and he was planning to go there via Dubai. He was clear that Afghanistan had no future any more.

Both came to drop me off at the hotel, and on our way there my friend stopped at an Internet cafe for one last story he was following that evening. At the cafe, Afghans who had worked for the American government or for American or NATO troops during the twenty-year war were being given special immigrant visas (SIVs). The cafe was full of Afghan men, all dressed in their traditional attire, scrambling to apply for the SIV holding piles of documents and ready to shell out any amount in USD just to get the coveted visa. One of them told me, 'It is a matter of life and death.'

In July, about 1,200 interpreters and their family members were evacuated on flights from Kabul to Fort Lee, Virginia, and the US embassy in Kabul started expediting thousands of remaining applications. But in the absence of any organised evacuation by the US government, Americans in civil society institutions tried to fill the void and scrambled to save their Afghan associates. They began negotiating with countries such as Albania and Qatar to accept charter flights filled with Afghan passengers on a temporary basis. Journalists were getting desperate calls from their former fixers – only to find that the Priority 2, or P2, refugee programme created by the Biden administration to resettle Afghans who had worked for American media and non-profit organisations and the US Agency for International Development existed only on paper and nowhere else[11]. It was a painful situation.

Just as we reached the Serena, I saw two pickup trucks filled with Taliban fighters stationed at the entry and exit points of the hotel. My friends, being locals, left me at the gate and fled from the scene while I entered the fortified entrance with a blank face and numb demeanour. Some of the lackeys, mostly in their early twenties and thirties, looked at me as if I were some kind of museum piece walking in front of them. I felt numb, as I said, and at that point even turned deaf, I think. I could not hear anything or anybody. I walked into the reception area. It was filled from corner to corner with Taliban fighters. The chaps at the reception looked as if they were made of stone and the front office manager was looking at me angrily, as if rebuking me with his eyes for going out alone. I quickly went into my room and started packing up.

Eventually, Mullah Abdul Ghani Baradar, considered a 'victor' in America's two-decade war,[12] announced victory over Afghanistan. His coming back to the limelight in Afghanistan was a reflection of the failure of the war-torn country to come out of its gory past. But the main fear factor that tightly gripped Kabul that day was the fact that the Haqqani Network was calling the shots, giving two hoots to the Taliban bosses sitting in faraway Doha. This is because the Haqqani Network,

TALIBAN BACK IN KABUL

which is a part of the Taliban, is the most deadly element of the group. Sirajuddin Haqqani and his uncle, Khalil, are the founding members of the Haqqani Network, an Afghan Sunni Islamist militant organisation that constitutes the Taliban's most vicious segment. The US designated the Haqqani Network as a foreign terrorist organisation in 2012 and has announced millions of dollars as bounty for each member of the group.

Mullah Abdul Ghani Baradar, or Mullah Baradar, was later appointed by the new Taliban government as the 'deputy leader' of the Taliban government. Baradar rose to prominence after the death of Mullah Omar in 2013. Baradar quickly became the face of the Taliban, skilfully negotiating with the Americans the peace deal and eventually signing it on behalf of the Taliban under the former Donald Trump administration.[13] He is a key figure in the Taliban's political office in Doha, Qatar.

Back in my room I focused on my work and packing. I closed the curtains over the big and wide windows of my room and pressed the loose ends against the windows with the use of chairs so that the inside could not be seen at all. Since my room overlooked the main road, I could see the constant movement of convoys of pickup trucks to and from the Serena, packed with Taliban fighters waving their big white flags. Those civilians who were out on the streets with their rickety rifles to kill the Taliban had simply vanished. To see what was happening outside in greater detail, I switched off all the lights in my room and slowly opened the windows. What I saw shocked me to bits. Row after row of Taliban convoys were zipping by my window. Some of the fighters were on foot, loudly sloganeering while waving their white flags. All those cars, the families walking on the pavement, the fruit sellers . . . were all gone. The watchtower on the opposite road was now empty. A security guard used to be stationed there at all times since it was a government office. I told myself, 'This is not the Kabul where I landed.'

To distract myself from the fear that was now slowly and gradually engulfing me as the Taliban surrounded the entire hotel, I started filing my interview with Hekmatyar. I was transcribing his answers to me when, at around 1.45 a.m., I received a call from the lobby that a couple of Taliban men, along with one of the receptionists, were coming to check my room. I felt choked to the core. I called my husband immediately over WhatsApp and put him on hold until the three men arrived at my door and rang the bell. My legs had stopped moving by then and I was shaking. I took a look at my son's photograph for one final moment before opening the door. There they were — two Taliban men in their ragtag attire, with best-of-the-class rifles on their shoulders. One of them looked at me and said nothing. They asked the receptionist to ask me if anyone was there in the room with me. I answered in the negative. They refused to believe me and one of them walked right into the room. However, he did not go into the main space but made a U-turn and left. I shut the door immediately and blacked out for a few seconds. My husband was holding on at the other end and finally disconnected when he was told the ordeal had ended. I stayed up the rest of the night, hoping to catch the Air India (AI 0244) flight back home.

9

Will I Die Today?

16 August 2021

The clock struck 3 a.m. I dozed off for an hour but got jolted out of of my chair as an American Chinook flew over the hotel at a very low height. For a second, in that drowsy state, I thought that perhaps bombing had started. I got ready in seconds and went downstairs with my luggage for the checkout. Another Indian journalist from a leading English national daily in India and I had planned to go to the airport in the same cab since we were booked on the same flight. We had both planned the previous evening to leave for the airport by 4 a.m. to avoid the rush and also the Taliban checkposts, which were slowly cropping up everywhere in the city.

I reached the lobby, and he too arrived at around the same time. We both settled our bills, readied our luggage and were preparing to leave, under the watchful eyes of the Taliban fighters who had been sitting in the lobby since the previous evening. My journalist friend had arranged for the cab, but it was delayed as the driver had difficulties coming out of his home. Meanwhile, I settled my bills and also deposited the SIM card given to me by my local driver there when I had landed in Kabul on 8 August. We were asked to wait beside the

WILL I DIE TODAY? 113

reception manager at the rear side of the reception area to 'avoid attracting' the Taliban fighters. We – especially I, being a woman – were asked not to look directly at them. Both of us waited for the driver to come, and just as we were moving our luggage to a side a bunch of about seventy Taliban fighters moved behind us as if they were following us. We kept our calm and sat down. One of them was adjusting his rifle, which was hanging casually from his shoulders, while another was cleaning the barrel of his. Yet another fellow was smiling at us, and that made us more stiff.

I remember telling myself, 'There is no escape now. They are everywhere now.' Just how rapidly the Taliban grabbed Kabul was baffling, I thought, as till less than twenty-four hours back people were confident that a deal would happen between them and that the Republic would remain. Just then, a security officer of the Serena came running towards us to tell us our taxi had arrived. We ran out of the hotel. I then realised that I had left my suitcase behind in the lobby. However, I was not allowed to step inside the hotel and the security manager brought the suitcase out himself and loaded it into the cab, and we left. It was pitch-dark. The taxi driver told us that the Taliban was creating checkpoints at every 100 metres on Kabul's main roads. He was kind and warm. He was risking his life to do his duty. The route from Serena to the airport looked unrecognisable. I had traversed this route just a few days back, and within just a few hours everything looked so completely different. There was no doubt that Afghanistan was not the same any more.

Finally, we were nearly at the airport. It seemed extraordinarily crowded from what it had been just a couple of days back when I had come to the very same place to catch a flight to Mazar. The car was stopped from entering the airport so we got down at the main gate of the Hamid Karzai International Airport, on the main road. We started walking towards the international terminal, which is adjacent to the domestic terminal. While we were making our way to the building we saw people frantically running towards the main area. Some of them were wearing casual home clothes. Women and men were running aimlessly, children and toddlers looked scared and confused. Everyone kept running and everything looked extremely odd. The distance between the main gate and the terminal is 70–80 metres, so we were still not aware of what was going on inside. Why so many people? Where were they going? We had walked about 40 metres ahead before we realised what we had got ourselves into. As we moved a little further, we encountered a monstrous crowd consisting of women, men, children and elders, clogging the main entrance to the international terminal, all surging towards the roundabout that divides the terminals, the roundabout that bore the signage 'I LOVE KABUL', and Taliban fighters were repeatedly circling that roundabout in their Humvees (all-terrain vehicles) shooting incessantly into the air. There were about eight to ten Humvees circling the roundabout. They were screaming into a loudspeaker threatening people, asking them to go back home and not crowd the airport. Both of us froze. That's

WILL I DIE TODAY? 115

when we realised that the world had changed. There was absolutely no way we could go anywhere near the terminal, forget about entering the main airport building.

Somehow we jostled our way towards the outermost building that was attached to the terminal. There we found blood smeared all over, from the chairs to the floor. The floor had bloodstains that seemed to indicate that someone had been dragged out of that room after being shot. We kept asking around, inquiring about what was going on, but nobody seemed to have any clue. One person told us that the Taliban had shut down the airport and was not letting anybody go in since many had tried to flee the country the night before when the Taliban was taking over the reins of the country. We immediately started calling our respective families. The gunfire was so loud that even they could hear it on the other side.

The Taliban was spraying bullets towards the sky and sometimes even in the direction of the people to control the swelling crowd. The main alley leading up to the terminals was lined with trees and there was a stretch of rose garden in between. We sat on the edge of the narrow pavement that ran in the middle of the alley and tried to put our heads together as to what to do next. All this while I had been using a local SIM card and local Wi-Fi and had never bothered to activate international roaming on my Airtel number from India. But that day was different. We felt that either both of us or one of us might get killed at the airport that day. Somehow, my international roaming facility had stopped. Back in India, my husband got my Airtel international roaming activated, and someone called Gill at Airtel customer care proved to be unusually efficient. He made sure my package started working without any delay.

I then started frantically calling the Indian embassy in Kabul. The person at the other end sounded so calm I wondered if he was in some other Afghanistan that I was not aware of. My journalist colleague also tried to explain the situation to them, but in vain. The embassy people kept saying that the Air India plane would land and we had to somehow make our way to the aircraft. Finding no way out of our situation, we kept sitting with our luggage on the edge of the pavement, hiding ourselves behind the rose bushes that lined the alley. There were many other large families with us – tense, worried and anxious about what lay ahead for them.

As the sun rose higher, the Taliban manning the gates and the terminal became more ferocious because the crowds were only swelling and hundreds of men were constantly trying to run up to the tarmac braving the bullets, the whips and whatnot. Some even jumped the high walls covered with barbed wires to run up to the tarmac and board any aircraft that would take them to whichever faraway land it was headed to. It was an excruciatingly painful sight. The burqa-clad women, who could not jump those walls, handed over their children to their husbands, brothers and fathers so that at least their young could make it even if they did not. As the hours passed, the road got filled with bullet shells and bloodstains. The Taliban men also began to look exhausted and nervous as they were not used to seeing or managing such a gigantic rush of people. These men were quite young, the oldest no more than twenty-five or twenty-seven, and this was their first experience of managing such a massive crowd in the country's capital, who were defiant of them.

We called the Indian embassy officials again, and officials at the Ministry of External Affairs too. We were told that the embassy could not send a car to pick us up from the airport and take us to the embassy since the Taliban had blocked all the roads and lives could not be put in danger. Another option now struck out . . .

At about 9.45 a.m., the Taliban men removed all the Humvees from the roundabout and the situation seemed to have eased. But we could hear firing going on inside the terminals. As we sat there helplessly, we met a beautiful-looking couple with three children walking towards the terminal. Seeing us sitting the way we were and taking note of the commotion, the man asked us what had happened. The couple did not seem very perturbed. They had valid visas and tickets for Turkey, where the husband worked as a contractor. He had come to Afghanistan to take his family back with him to Turkey. After some exchange of pleasantries, they faded into the crowd.

At around 11 a.m., the Taliban announced they are shutting down all airports across Afghanistan. I Face-timed my husband, who found out from his sources that the Air India flight had been cancelled. In the background I saw my son singing 'Jana Gana Mana' before the Indian tricolour as his school was conducting an online Independence Day programme. It was surreal.

I called the Indian embassy again, and this time an official there told us to walk up to the technical area of the airport. He said it was nearby and would take us five to ten minutes to get there on foot. We thought that would be a better option than waiting for a bullet to hit us. But there were bullets everywhere. By now the Taliban had deboarded the Humvees and had spread into every nook and corner of the airport. They were hiding in the corners, or behind pillars, or inside the check-in booths and were shooting people. But the Afghans kept running helter-skelter under the raining bullets. Some made it and climbed up the walls to reach the tarmac, while some got shot at and continued to walk on or got instantly killed. It was as if the Jallianwala Bagh tragedy was being played out in front of my eyes – only the size of the population and the place was bigger and the enemy was not some foreigner but one of their own.

Now that it was confirmed that the embassy officials would not be able to come to the airport to save us, we started walking towards the technical area of the airport. We were crossing the main baggage check-in area when a bout of firing began. We managed to sit on chairs attached to the wall of the terminal. It was an area closed on top and open on two opposite sides. Realising that we were heading nowhere, we sat down to eat. My friend was carrying some snacks. He had a Haldiram's packet of moong dal. We ate that in the midst of the constant firing going on outside. We even took a selfie there and sent it to our families telling them we were fine. Deep down, I also felt this could be the last image of mine for my close ones to cherish. By now we were completely trapped in the Taliban area. We saw men chasing young boys who were trying to flee, dragging them along the floor or even shooting them brutally in front of their parents. The families could not even cry or display any emotion. The men of the family began removing the dead or injured bodies of their loved ones and casting them to a side so that they did not invite unnecessary attention from the Taliban who had gone completely berserk and could shoot anyone. They did not even let the families grieve the dead.

The embassy was now telling me to go back to the Serena and my colleague to head towards the embassy. But we decided we would not go in different directions and instead planned to head towards the embassy together. It was already nearing 1 p.m. and the crowd outside the terminals was getting thinner and thinner as the Taliban men were chasing everyone out of the airport premises. At that point everything went blurry and we couldn't exactly fathom what was happening. Every second we were fighting death, which was right in front of us, playing hide-and-seek. Finally, after almost six hours of our ordeal at the airport, we decided to move towards the embassy. I was completely unsure of what would happen next, but this much I could sense – that evacuation of the Indian embassy was in fact happening, even though we were not told about it.

Risking everything, we decided to exit the airport, which meant walking out of the airport the same way we had come in. People were also complaining about local cabs not operating, so we had no clue how to make it to the embassy. But we had to somehow leave the airport. We came out of the corridor of the domestic terminal where we had been hiding for half an hour and started to walk towards the main gate with a poker face. By then the Taliban had put up a small barricade to check the travel documents of those who had come to the airport, to ensure that nobody was trying to flee. Anyone without travel documents was being beaten up mercilessly and even shot. I hid my engagement ring and watch inside my handbag, and also the book I had planned to read on the plane – Ahmed Rashid's *Taliban* – under a pile of wires and power banks inside my handbag. Just as we reached the ubiquitous checkpoint, three Taliban men dropped everything they were doing. They looked at us blankly.

Before they could ask us anything we said we were from India, where there is Bollywood. One of them asked me as he checked both my handbags, 'Shah Rukh Khan?' I said yes, and he let me go. I still don't know what exactly he meant when he asked me, 'Shah Rukh Khan?', but we were just too relieved to have crossed the first hurdle to ponder over it. While people were leaving the airport in hordes, creating a rough queue on the pavements leading up to the main gate, four or five Taliban men came running down the road between the pavements and started shooting at the crowd.

This was in order to control another crowd that had gatecrashed into the airport. It happened just as we were about to reach the gate. Both of us kept walking. Suddenly the man walking behind me got shot in the leg and fell to the ground. Seeing that, I screamed and stopped walking. I hid behind my suitcase, as if it was some kind of shield. A Taliban man came up and stood right in front of us. Around us were women running, tearing up their burqas that were drenched in blood. There were shoes strewn all over the road.

By then I had lost all sanity and was just screaming, when all of a sudden a man dressed in the traditional Afghan Kandahar-style Pashtun dress, who had come to the airport to flee the country, grabbed my hands and started running towards the main gate, leading me along. I felt too choked with panic to speak and looked at him curiously as we kept running towards the main gate. He looked at me and yelled 'madad'. I said nothing but realised that he was genuinely helping me. We reached the main gate. It was clear that Kabul had been turned upside down. The man helped us cross the road and tried negotiating with the local taxis; the drivers would take one look at our faces and refuse to take us. Ultimately, this man managed to convince a taxi driver to drop us at the embassy for 500 Afghani. We boarded the taxi and left for our destination. Our saviour waved at us and then ran back towards the airport. I do not remember his face but only his long hair, and who knows if he is still alive. But he will always remain an angel for me.

The taxi ride was another ordeal. Every 100 metres we were stopped and checked, and our driver panicked and yelled at me every time this happened. I was asked to cover my head and we had to act as a couple so that the Taliban wouldn't know that I was with two men who were not related to me. I covered my head with my dupatta and kept my head down throughout. The journey of fifteen minutes took us thirty. I felt I was in a completely different place from where I had been just a few hours ago. How could a city look so different in a matter of few hours, I wondered. Finally, we reached the main road leading up to the embassy, and there waited for us another hurdle. This one looked impossible to cross.

It was about 2 p.m. when we reached the main barricade of the embassy, which until 8 August, when I last visited, had been manned by the Afghan police. Now it was being managed by the Taliban. There were six of them at the barricade. They did not look even remotely as crass and rookie as the ones at the airport. The current lot looked more reserved and avoided any kind of confrontation, probably because they were posted at a VVIP location, an enclave that housed the embassies of the some of key countries. The Indian embassy was at the end of that enclave in a remote corner, and that made it more vulnerable to any kind of targeting.

Besides the Taliban, there was another crisis that we witnessed there. There were thirty to fifty young Afghan men and women who were fighting with

WILL I DIE TODAY?

the Taliban men so they could enter the enclave and speak to someone at the Indian embassy. Their passports were with the embassy as they had applied for an Indian visa for various reasons, but mainly for educational purposes. One particular sight still haunts me — a young girl fell at our feet and started weeping profusely. She was in her late twenties and was there with her mother, trying to reach the embassy. Both had applied for an Indian visa to visit the girl's brother who was languishing in a jail somewhere in India. She was not aware which prison her brother was lodged in. I tried to speak to her, but the situation was getting from bad to worse there. The Taliban was threatening to even kill them if any of those youngsters tried to speak to us or tried to enter the embassy by latching on to us.

Just then, a group of men approached us to speak to the Taliban men. We were ourselves exhausted and had no idea what to do. We kept calling the embassy to at least send a car to that point, which was about 1 kilometre away. Eventually a car was sent, but it was turned back by the Taliban. I tried to negotiate with the Taliban but they were not ready to relent. Each of them was holding a Kalashnikov and a grenade launcher. But I was not ready to give up. I had a little child waiting for me back home, whom I had promised I would come back. NO MATTER WHAT!!!

So, without thinking twice I walked straight towards them and called for their boss, who knew rather good English. If they killed us on the road it would become a huge issue for them, I said. So it would be best for everyone to allow us to enter the embassy. I also showed them the WhatsApp message that Suhail Shaheen had sent me, assuring me that nothing untoward would happen to foreigners and journalists. They read that message and allowed both of us to enter the enclave through the iron-beamed gates. But there was one condition – we would not turn to look back at them but would walk right to the embassy, or they would shoot us. We walked on, and a little before we entered the embassy we found a car being driven by a local worker there, and he dropped us at the gate.

When we entered the gates our luggage was taken away for scanning and we were told it would be given to us only at the time of our leaving. Inside the embassy everything was packed and ready for loading into the Land Cruisers, which were owned by the embassy. We were given whatever lunch was available in the canteen and were taken to meet the ambassador, who was in his room waiting to hear the entire story of our ordeal at the airport. We gave him all the granular details. Finally we were brought outside, where some kind of drill was going on with the Indo-Tibetan Border Police (ITBP) personnel deployed there to provide security to the diplomatic staff. Apparently, the embassy had even held a flag-hoisting ceremony celebrating Independence Day, even though the intelligence agencies told them to leave the country a couple of days before. According to a source, whom I met in the course of my research for this book, Afghan defence officials had been asking the Indian embassy to evacuate by 12–13 August. But India refused to pay heed to the inputs.

Anyhow, we were all huddled up in cars lined up to take the embassy staff out and were told we would be leaving for the airport soon. Meanwhile, an official sharply rebuked me, thinking I would be tweeting out images of what was going on inside the embassy, which I never did. But I think he was probably seized by panic, as he issued a whip for our phones to be taken away. So for the next three or four hours we were left without our phones and I could not talk to anyone, even my family. Finally, after a lot of pleading on our part our phones were given back to us. Needless to say, my family was petrified with worry.

There were about twenty-four Land Cruisers, and we were seated ten to twelve in one, all sticking to each other. There we sat for almost six hours. Finally, as the sun went down, we were told that the evacuation had been delayed yet again. There could be an airlift, in which case not everyone would be taken. And, of course, my turn would come late, or so I was told. All hell broke loose for me when I heard that. I had not reached the embassy fighting death every second of the way only to hear this. Basically, there was zero assurance given to us about our return to India.

Around 7 p.m., we were asked to freshen up for dinner and we were provided rooms in the new residential quarters at the embassy that had come up only a few months back within the old embassy campus. They were sparklingly fresh and new. I was still very shaken by the ordeal I had been through and at my being on my own to save myself. I thought to myself . . . I knew this would happen and that such a moment would come when I would repent leaving the hotel to catch the damn Air India flight in the first place. I thought about how I had tried to convince my office not to push me to come back because the situation was just not right for it, and how I could have done things some other way . . .

I called some of my Afghan friends about the situation outside, and they also seemed to have no clue about what the Taliban was going to do next. I told them how I had managed to negotiate with the Taliban in whatever little way I could, whether at the airport or to enter the embassy area. They thought it was brave of me to deal with them and not give up. I guess I got the courage for all that from looking at those hundreds and thousands of families who faced war every single day but moved on with life as if nothing were happening.

I called home. Everyone was in a sombre mood as all hopes of my coming back appeared to be fading away. It was now around 8 p.m., and our ordeal had begun at 4 a.m. when we left the Serena. Suddenly I felt tremendously hungry and drowsy, and home seemed far away. The spotless white rooms that still smelled of fresh paint and the brown furniture all seemed inappropriate in that situation. Nothing seemed correct. As I tried to close my eyes, my phone buzzed. On the other end was someone whom I have always respected for her utter professionalism, a true leader who is much more than an ex-boss to me. She remains an inspiration for me and will always be one. The powerful woman that she is, she told me in clear words that the embassy would be evacuated that night itself. She was sitting miles and miles away, yet she knew perfectly well what she was talking about. She told me that both the NSAs of the US and India, Jake Sullivan and Ajit Doval, respectively, had a discussion and an evacuation plan has been finalised. As per the plan, the Indian Air Force (IAF) would be allowed to use the technical part of the Kabul airport manned by the US troops. Her words calmed me deep within, and I was back to my roaring self, deciding not to be afraid, or at least not show outwardly what was going on within.

In about ten minutes we were asked to come down to the main area for dinner. But when we assembled outside the building where we were put up, we were asked to rush back and get all our belongings out as we were finally 'evacuating'. For the first time in all my hours at the embassy I was hearing this word. The challenge was not so much in fitting so many people into the twenty-four or so Land Cruisers the Indian embassy had as it was to get all those hundreds of black trunks that contained sensitive documents all the way to India. But the ITBP personnel did an immensely efficient job of managing the embassy staff, the non-embassy people like us, the sensitive luggage and, of course, themselves. The young ITBP women who sat with me for hours and hours told me how they had reached Kabul hoping it would be one of their 'dream postings' but could never step out of the embassy premises as the situation was not conducive for that. While we were again huddled up inside the car with no signs of our leaving for the airport, we discussed how fine Kabuli blankets were and how delicate the design of Afghan women's clothing was . . . we were just killing time, the reality being that we were not sure whether we were going to come out of the situation dead or alive.

10

Back Home, with a Bit of Afghanistan in Me

17 August 2021

I badly needed to get home now that I was forced to come back from Afghanistan, but here I was languishing inside the Indian embassy in Kabul, where hope was at its lowest ebb. The embassy was busy packing up and I felt neither here nor there. I was desperate to go back to the Serena and continue with my reporting but I was helpless. Moreover, for no fault of mine the embassy officials snatched my phones away recklessly thinking that I was taking photos of the embassy to use them on social media. To date I haven't done so. For nearly two hours the phone was with them and I had no way to connect with the world outside. Around midnight, we were given the green signal by the Taliban to finally make our exit and head towards the airport. I got to know from one of my most reliable sources, who called me on WhatsApp, that an IAF plane would shortly be landing in the technical area of the Kabul airport and that we would be brought back in it. But that would happen only if we were able to reach the airport safely. There were high chances of the Taliban launching an assault on the entire convoy, and the biggest threat was from the Haqqanis, who by then had started to tighten their grip on the Afghan capital. This was the reason why the ambassador was made to sit in a strategically placed car in our convoy.

It was way past midnight when we were ordered to move. The gigantic gates of the embassy were flung open, and there they were right outside the gate – middle-aged Taliban men, about twenty to thirty of them, waving at us with what I thought was a slight tinge of a smile on their rugged faces. I thought it was all good, but I was totally wrong. The young men at the gates with whom I had negotiated hours back were actually all giving us stern looks, as if they were unhappy that we were leaving and wanted to harass us some more. Every other building on that road had its interior lights off, its main gates open, and was all empty. I wondered how every other embassy had evacuated except India. What had happened? Was there some kind of intelligence failure? At that moment nothing seemed right or wrong, true or false . . . everything looked blurry.

The roads were empty and had only Taliban men. Not a single other soul was present on the road. All the houses went dark and the street lights seemed to have become dimmer. Was Kabul looking like Kandahar? Or was I dreaming? The roundabouts were filled with Taliban checkposts, manned by fifteen to twenty of their men. At every one of them we were stopped. The men would knock aggressively on the windows and

BACK HOME, WITH A BIT OF AFGHANISTAN IN ME 131

ask the same questions of everyone. The drill was that all the cars would move in tandem and not one would leave the convoy and move ahead even if it was given clearance from the Taliban to do so. The traffic police, the checkposts of the former Afghan police, had all vanished in a matter of hours. Images of Kabul under the previous Taliban era flashed in front of my eyes. This was not the Kabul of 2021 where I had landed ten days back; it was maybe the Kabul of 1996. That night spoke to me as my car slowly inched towards the technical area of the airport where the American forces were stationed. It seemed to me that Afghanistan was slipping from the hands of time, and I feared its people would be abandoned while the big powers continued to play their war games in their country on some or other pretext.

A distance that would have taken thirty minutes during rush hour took us two hours as the Taliban kept stopping us at every checkpoint scrutinising the entire convoy. Finally, at 2.30 a.m., we reached the technical area of the airport, which was still under the control of US/NATO troops. The entire convoy stood at the main entry for hours. This was very close to Abbey Gate, where there would be a suicide bomb attack on 26 August, killing 170 Afghans and 13 US service personnel. As we reached the gate, our cars were lined up bumper to bumper, waiting for the authorities to open the gates and allow them entry. I had dozed off on the way but got jolted out of my slumber when a burqa-clad lady insanely banged on my window begging me to take her family inside. As we waited for hours for the gates to open, the monstrous crowd of helpless and ordinary Afghans crowded the gates and our convoy. It was not as easy as I had thought it would be. It seemed that along with my body my mind had also gone numb. Despite the ordeal, I did not feel hungry and did not feel the need to go to the washroom, I did not even clearly remember what I was thinking during that long wait. The only thing I remember is staring at the Afghan people helplessly. Despite being armed with all kinds of permissions, we were not allowed inside the technical area immediately. And the crowd around our convoy was swelling so rapidly that in order to bring it under control the Taliban began flogging the men, women and children mercilessly while we waited for the gates to open. It was becoming a security threat for us and the Taliban could see that our convoy had become a centre of attraction for the crowd desperate to go into the airport.

Finally, when the gates were opened, the crowd was brutally stopped from going inside by the Taliban. Our convoy went in, with the US soldiers looking on. They were all dressed in combat attire and seemed ready to face any kind of potential attack from the Taliban or even the ISIS. The technical area of the airport was separated from the regular area of the airport by barbed wire and the entire boundary was manned by US forces. The area was lit with stadium lights and there was a massive commotion going on inside as Washington was carrying out its own evacuation operations there. Our cars were ordered to be parked in a corner of the tarmac which was mostly being used to register people who were to be evacuated by the Americans. Here we all got out. Humvees, trucks and all kinds of equipment were strewn across the huge area. We were asked to line up and submit our passports for stamping, which happened quickly. Following this we were asked to wait as the IAF aircraft that would take us had not yet landed.

As we kept waiting in that makeshift waiting area that the American troops had built for themselves over the course of the twenty-year war they were fighting there, I noticed several Afghan families waiting to board a flight, and they all seemed relieved and happy. The waiting area was lit up with tubelights and had an abundant supply of bottled mineral water. A young woman in her early twenties asked me for a pen as she filled in document after document seeking a safe passage for herself and her family out of her country, her home, her entire life back in Afghanistan. And maybe forever. The Americans who had once promised to give her a safe and secure life that would be free from terror and also to turn Afghanistan into some desirable country were now giving passes to several hundreds and thousands like her to run away from that very country.

As we both waited for our respective turns to leave, I started casually chatting with her, careful to not alarm her too much. She looked distraught but was overall in a jovial mood as she was content that her father, who had served at the US embassy as a 'special staff', was able to procure an SIV on time and also evacuate his entire family without facing any torture at the hands of the Taliban. She said the Taliban had come to their apartment the previous night looking for those who had worked with the Ghani government or the NATO troops. They had killed some of them and flogged some others, she said. But her father had told his family to pack their bags and had brought them away on the night of 14 August, when the key city of Mazar was captured. Mazar was like a fortress, compared to which Kabul was easier to capture with nobody to defend it. He had sensed it then, she told me proudly. Her father had always been considered the best by the Americans when it came to gathering intelligence.

I asked her what was next. She said she was eagerly looking forward to continuing her studies in America along with her two brothers and her younger sister. Her mother planned to cook Afghan delicacies for the Afghan community in the US, and her father would work closely with the 'Americans'. Her plans seemed very clear, as if someone had handed over her life's roadmap to her. We promised to stay in touch as we exchanged mobile numbers. The last time we spoke, the family was somewhere in Canada and she was still looking for a college to join. She never told me how she ended up in Canada because she was supposed to live in the US. They did not have a house but lived in a refugee area. Her siblings were going to school and she was helping her mother cook. She sounded depressed and morose and cried for the 'good life' she had back in Afghanistan. Had it not for the Taliban, she said, she would have never left her 'beautiful Afghanistan'. To many young women like her who were born after the Taliban was ousted by the Americans, Afghanistan was like a dream where one felt safe. There was Afghan culture, yet there was also an American way of life, where women enjoyed freedom and where jobs were being generated.

'Nayanima Basu.' An American woman in charge of visa issues at the airport called out my name. My passport was ready and I could now board the flight to India. All of us on that flight, including the embassy staff, were taken to the tarmac in a bus. Needless to say, everyone was in a jubilant mood, but something in me didn't allow me to share the same feeling. The faces of those young men and women near the embassy gates, of that old lady who smiled at me while I walked through the gates . . . she thought I would take her with me, but she also realised that I was helpless, yet she smiled at me as if she was blessing me. Her son, she had said, was lodged in a jail in India. On the way to our aircraft, I saw the sight of ten to fifteen American choppers parked together. All appeared damaged. At that time I thought it was due to the impact of the war. I only came to know later that the Americans deliberately dismantled and broke all their war machinery so that they would be useless if they fell into the hands of the Taliban. Finally, the buses stopped in front of a massive C-17 Globemaster of the IAF, which looked as grand as the mountains bordering the main Kabul airport.

Needless to mention here, the expression of relief everyone had on their faces, the glow of happiness they had from knowing they were heading home after the ordeal they had been through, which could have been completely avoided, is indescribable.

As a reporter who is passionate about defence and international relations, I was thrilled to board the C-17 Globemaster, to be inside this beast which seemed to swallow us all up. Even after everyone had boarded it, it looked empty. It was my palace on wheels for that day, as it was taking me to my family, my son. The plane had two decks. The inside looked like a jungle of wires but it was capable of accommodating an entire village in its belly. We were told by the officials accompanying us that we should be grateful for the craft we got because apparently the C-17s that the Americans were using for their evacuation didn't have seats attached. I wonder what the point was of mentioning this at all.

Had I not been booked on that Air India flight that day, I wouldn't have pushed myself into the jaws of death. As we waited for take-off, a journalist friend, not from India, who had stayed back in Kabul and continued to report from there for a few more months, messaged me to say that the Taliban was meeting the media at the Serena's reception area and this would be followed by a press conference, their first since coming to power. I was missing it. That feeling of missing something so key by just a few hours, the void that it created in me as a professional, continues to bother me to this day.

As we took off at 7.18 a.m. (Kabul time), I told myself that I would be back in Afghanistan. We first landed in Jamnagar, Gujarat, at around 11 a.m. (IST) for refuelling. Little did I know that there would still be several hours to go before I could see the face of my family, especially my little son, who was eagerly waiting for my return. We had to deboard at Jamnagar, where we were taken to a massive hangar at the Jamnagar air force base. Representatives of the local government were already present there to 'welcome' us and give us each a packet of sweets, which I refused. They then asked us to hold up a banner with Prime Minister Narendra Modi's life-sized photos printed on it. Some of the Indian families travelling with us, who were also evacuating Afghanistan, cried 'Modiji' and 'Bharat Mata ki Jai'. Honestly, I was too lost in my thoughts to do any of that. So I politely refused to be a part of that photo-op. I was more concerned that while the world's greatest travesty was unfolding, I was not able to write or send my reports. We were then served lunch. There were only chairs, and no tables, inside the hangar, which had turned into a heat chamber. The ambassador even addressed the local press there. The rest of us were not invited to that media conference and we came to know about it only after it was over. The Indian ambassador to Afghanistan at the time, Rudrendra Tandon, who was accompanied by the then deputy chief of mission, S. Raghuram, said at the press conference, 'I am very happy and I think the whole mission is very happy that it's finally over and that we are back home safely and securely without any accidents or harm to any one of us . . . Our policy was anyone who reached the embassy was taken into the embassy. I don't know how they managed inside the embassy but we ensured that they were safe, secure and there was an avenue for an exit.'[1]

After a while, the tedious process of stamping passports began, and that took almost two hours. We finally boarded the aircraft at around 2.45 p.m. and took off at 3.20 p.m. to land at the Hindon Air Force Station in Ghaziabad, Uttar Pradesh, on the outskirts of Delhi. We were told that a battery of media was waiting for us there, which, like the banner and the gifts in Jamnagar, I wanted to completely avoid. I felt bad as they belonged to the same profession as I did, and had I been in their place I would have been doing exactly what they were, but at that moment I did not want to be the story. After reaching Hindon we were once again made to sit inside a hangar, where some snacks were served and some more photo-ops created. But I wanted to go home, so I kept asking the embassy officials for a shuttle or a cab to drop me to the main gate of the air force base, since it was a huge place and it's not easy to find transport. Besides, this was a sensitive area and I did not want any more problems. I finally managed to get someone to drop me to the gate, where I saw hundreds of cameras waiting to take bytes from those who had returned. I respect my profession, and I thought it would be better if the reporters spoke to the people who had lived in Afghanistan for a number of years and who had a story to tell. I exited the gates and called for an Ola and got to my home in Noida. That was when I felt truly safe.

I will end the story of my journey with what my then managing editor, Y.P. Rajesh, told me at the time, the meaning of which I did not grasp until I sat down and decided to write this book: 'The escape from Kabul is your own story.'

Epilogue

The Taliban's comeback and takeover of Afghanistan is of huge significance for India's national security, as it is for the rest of the world. For India, the comeback of the Taliban means yet another challenge in its immediate neighbourhood, in addition to the security threats it has been contending with for decades from Pakistan and its all-weather ally China. The US, when it started the war in Afghanistan, had made it clear that it 'should not and will not' engage in 'forever wars'. It is based on this principle that Washington brought its war in Afghanistan to an abrupt end, even if that meant a chaotic and rushed withdrawal of its troops from the war-torn country on 31 August 2021, which led to the collapse of the Republic that America itself had created in 2001 by ousting the Taliban. The withdrawal paved the way to power for the hardliners, who continue to have links with Al-Qaeda, the elimination of which was the US's original aim post the 9/11 attacks.

With the coming back of the Taliban to power in Afghanistan, the situation has once again become complex. The twenty-year-long war has failed to bring peace. If anything, the hasty withdrawal of international troops in the absence of a solid roadmap for Afghanistan has only hardened its image as the world's most favourite battlefield where mega powers like the US and Russia come to assert influence and expand their presence in the subcontinent. Whether we talk about 1979, when the Soviets invaded Afghanistan, or 2001, when the Americans declared their war on terror and attacked Afghanistan, the ideological clash between the US and the erstwhile USSR continued to wreak havoc in Afghanistan, destroying the rich ethnocultural hub it was once was.

It was in 1979 that the then US president Jimmy Carter activated channels of communication with those who were fighting against the pro-Soviet regime in Kabul. This he did on the suggestion of his NSA, Zbigniew Brzezinski, who believed that if the US openly and directly came to the aid of these fighters it would 'induce a Soviet military intervention'. Thus began the saga of jihad in Afghanistan, fomented by the US, in collaboration with Saudi Arabia and Pakistan. The US would arm the Afghan fighters, or Mujahideens, with weapons bought from the communist government of Czechoslovakia. The Carter regime also started 'buying arms for the Mujahideen from the Soviet army in Afghanistan, because that army was increasingly corrupt', Brzezinski said in an interview later on.[1]

The Soviet occupation of Afghanistan eventually came to a symbolic end on 15 February 1989 when the last commander of the Soviet army crossed over to Uzbekistan over the 'Friendship Bridge'. In an uncanny similarity, the end of the US's war in Afghanistan was marked by the departure of the last American soldier Major General Chris Donahue on 30 August 2021. What

EPILOGUE

the rest of the world does not fathom is the immense and monumental pain, torture and dehumanising phase Afghanistan went through in this thirty-two-year period. While the Soviets ravaged the country for ten years from 1979 to 1989 by interfering in their internal politics and backing those political leaders who believed in communism, the Americans ransacked this beautiful, culturally rich nation for twenty years; and in between generations of Afghans were born and perished under the smell of gunpowder. Foreign fighters came in and went out of Afghanistan, but the country could never experience true peace as it had become the global hub of jihad activities, attracting radical Muslims from all over the world. Eventually, Afghanistan became a terror haven feeding extremist outfits in Pakistan, and this continues to cause instability in South Asia.

More than two years since the return of the Taliban in Kabul, Afghanistan continues to remain a geostrategic nightmare for the world. The Joe Biden administration has been subjected to a series of investigations by the Republicans into what even some quarters in the US believe has been a chaotic withdrawal. In April 2023, Congressman James Comer had said, 'The Biden Administration was tragically unprepared for the Afghanistan withdrawal and their decisions in the region directly resulted in a national security and humanitarian catastrophe . . . Every relevant department and agency should be prepared to cooperate and provide all requested information.'[2] The Republicans questioned the Biden administration mainly on two accounts – first, why US intelligence said the Ghani government in Kabul would continue to function, and second, why the US military was not better equipped to handle such a catastrophe as the fall of Kabul to the Taliban. To this day these questions remain unanswered.

The Taliban has strengthened its position more firmly across all of Afghanistan since it took over the country. The government is still technically an interim administration. The Taliban's ranks have swelled and its policies have become louder and sharper, while resistance against it has died a silent death. To begin with, the Taliban has made it clear that it will continue to rule in the same manner it did previously. Despite severe threats and warnings from the international community, including from countries such as Saudi Arabia and the UAE, the Taliban continues to prevent women from getting a formal education. Since its takeover, the number of secret schools for girls has grown at least tenfold, according to unofficial figures. But even these secret schools are not safe from attacks by the Taliban. In March 2023, the Taliban did the inevitable. While it came as a shock to many, many others knew this development would only be a matter of time. The Taliban apprehended the world-renowned young Afghan education activist Matiullah Wesa from his house in a midnight raid. Wesa, thirty, had shot to overnight fame when he began working for Afghan girls' education rights, something he had been doing dedicatedly for fourteen years through his own NGO, PenPath. He continued his work even

EPILOGUE

after the Taliban's return in August 2021. After seven months in prison, Wesa was released by the Taliban in October 2023.

For about six to seven months after the Taliban takeover of Kabul, the international community, including India, had high hopes that it would be pushed back. Indian intelligence agencies went into hyperactive mode, thinking the anti-Taliban National Resistance Front (NRF) would be able to repel the Taliban and started providing clandestine support to the front. The NRF was fighting the Taliban from Panjshir Valley, which had been its bastion for decades. After all, this was the same Panjshir Valley from where Ahmed Shah Massoud had come into the global limelight. Massoud, known as the 'Lion of Panjshir', was assassinated on 9 September 2001, two days before the World Trade Centre attacks. Massoud had kept up a sustained campaign against the Taliban till he died. He could do so because countries like Russia, Iran and even India helped him generously with aid.[3] But today the situation is different. Massoud's son, Ahmad Massoud, has not been able to garner the same kind of international aid or support today, say some of my Afghan friends. These friends are today scattered all over the world and are waiting for the call that will signal to them to get together as a united force to demolish the Taliban.

In September 2021, the Taliban claimed victory over Panjshir Valley, which was considered the last of the hold-out provinces. The Taliban's chief spokesperson Zabihullah Mujahid said, 'With this victory, our

THE FALL OF KABUL

country is completely taken out of the quagmire of war.' The operation to defeat the Panjshiris was carried out with perfect precision; the mighty Panjshiris were themselves taken by surprise at the strategy the Islamist fundamentalist group adopted. The 115-kilometre valley surrounded by rugged mountains, an hour and a half's drive from Kabul, was lost to the Taliban in no time as the latter came armed with all kinds of modern equipment left behind by the American and NATO troops. A report by the US Department of Defence Office of Inspector General said there was US-funded equipment worth $7.12 billion in the inventory of the former Afghan government when it collapsed, much of which has since been seized by the Taliban. This included military aircraft, ground vehicles, weapons and other military equipment. It is not known what condition the equipment is in, and the long-term operability of the vehicles is likely to deteriorate without US contractor maintenance.[4]

The US forces left behind an estimated eighty aircraft – whose control panels they broke before they left – in the technical area of the Hamid Karzai International Airport. These aircraft are believed to have been repaired by the Taliban later, according to local Afghan journalists, and used for air raids in certain pockets of the country that were believed to be holdouts of anti-Taliban movements. Also, nearly 70 per cent of the weapons owned by the American troops had been given to the Afghan forces over the last twenty years, and eventually ammunition worth $48 million fell into the hands of the Taliban.[5]

EPILOGUE

To come back to Panjshir Valley, it is not too difficult to understand why the anti-Taliban fighters were so quickly overcome. According to one of them, who is still involved with the NRF, this time they carried out aerial attacks in the valley, unlike the previous times, making it easier for them to target the pockets from where the fighters were launching their offensive. Panjshiris have also blamed the junior Massoud's lack of experience in fighting and his inability to garner funds and weapons as one of the primary reasons for their failure.

The NRF's head of foreign relations, Ali Nazary, who is believed to be living in the US currently, had said in an interview with the BBC on 26 August 2021, 'The Red Army, with its might, was unable to defeat us . . . And the Taliban also 25 years ago . . . they tried to take over the valley and they failed, they faced a crushing defeat.'[6] In another interaction with an international media outlet in September 2021, Nazary said, 'The Taliban propaganda machine is trying to divert attention, is trying to spread propaganda, to weaken morale in Kabul and elsewhere.'[7] But the truth is, this was a new Taliban, more powerful, more sophisticated in its training in modern weaponry . . . that was why they could fly their white flags, or *Shahadas*, with ease while Nazary and his boss Massoud left for the West, leaving the poor Panjshiris and a few local commanders to fend for themselves.

How the Taliban has been able to govern that country since taking it over has been the subject of much debate. The answer is a hard truth that cannot be ignored — the international community has clandestinely engaged with it while officially refusing to recognise its government. The hypocritical stance that the world has taken against the Taliban government in Afghanistan is beyond appalling. A couple of days after the takeover on 17 August, the Taliban held its first-ever press conference in the heart of Kabul. It was to tell the world that it wanted peaceful and amicable ties with other countries. Addressing hundreds of local and foreign journalists, Taliban spokesperson Zabihullah Mujahid, flanked by other Taliban leaders, said:

> We have expelled the foreigners and I would like to congratulate the whole nation on this . . . Freedom and independence seeking is a legitimate right of every nation. The Afghans also use their legitimate right after 20 years of struggle for freedom and for emancipating the country from occupation, this was our right and we achieved this right . . . We know that we have been undergoing really challenging periods and crises, a lot of mistakes that were made that were an advantage to the occupiers. We want to make sure that Afghanistan is not the field of conflict, a battlefield of conflict anymore . . . We don't want any internal enemies and any external enemies.[8]

The Taliban announced a general amnesty for all those who had worked for the previous Republic governments and said that women could also join them in running the country. Unfortunately, it did the opposite. The Taliban killed and executed not just former soldiers

EPILOGUE

147

who had worked under the Ghani government but also former diplomats and government officials, attacking them and their families, storming their houses, beating up the inhabitants and sometimes even killing them.

The Taliban also drew up a structure for an interim government at Arg Palace, which it announced on 7 September 2021. The country was officially declared an 'Islamic Emirate' and the government consisted only of men. The dreaded Taliban founder and UN-proscribed Mullah Mohammad Hassan Akhund was named the leader. Islamic clergymen would constitute the government of a country that had undergone a metamorphosis since they last ruled the land. Among the names of those who got positions in the government, one that stood out and shocked people living outside Afghanistan was that of the new interior minister. It was Sirajuddin Haqqani, the FBI-wanted leader of the Haqqani militant group, an elusive, dreaded and feared terrorist who hardly ever appeared in front of the camera. At the time, there were no credible photos of him, but a popular image showing a side view of his face covered with a brown shawl. Some said he hid his face as it was scarred from burns, while others said he was not alive and that this was an image of an imposter.

In February 2020, as the world was still coming to terms with the news that the US, then under President Donald Trump, would be signing a peace deal with the Taliban, the Haqqani supremo came up with an opinion piece in the *New York Times* titled, 'What We, the Taliban, Want'. In that searing piece he blamed the US left, right and centre for what it had done to Afghanistan and its people in the name of the war on terror even as he wrote in clear terms that just as Washington 'does not trust' the Taliban completely, the Taliban too would never trust America and its government. In that scathing article, he said:

> We did not choose our war with the foreign coalition led by the US. We were forced to defend ourselves. The withdrawal of foreign forces has been our first and foremost demand. That we today stand at the threshold of a peace agreement with the US is no small milestone . . . We are aware of the concerns and questions in and outside Afghanistan about the kind of government we would have after the foreign troops withdraw. My response to such concerns is that it will depend on a consensus among Afghans. We should not let our worries get in the way of a process of genuine discussion and deliberation free for the first time from foreign domination and interference.[9]

On 28 September 2021, the Taliban announced an expansion of the cabinet. Also, at this time the validity of the Afghan Constitution – Qanun Asasi Jumhuri Islami Afghanistan – promulgated in 2004[10] by a 502-member assembly in Kabul, which had vowed to give shape to a nation that would be both Islamic as well as democratic, began to be questioned. The 2004 Constitution was derived from the vestiges of the 1964 Constitution, which had abolished the monarchy and brought in a democratic outlook for Afghanistan.

EPILOGUE

The 2004 Constitution led to the exclusion of not only the Taliban but also failed to recognise the rich diversity of the country. This was widely seen as an anomaly in the history of Afghanistan. This exclusion was also seen to be an 'original sin'[11] as mentioned by Ahmed Rashid in his book *Descent into Chaos*. Under the 2004 Constitution, the legislative power of the state was formally vested in the two houses of the national assembly. The Taliban, after coming to power in August 2021, dissolved both houses and effectively abandoned the 2004 Constitution. Since then the Amir al-Mu'minin, who is considered the supreme leader of the nation, has enacted important legislation via decrees, while other matters have been legislated via the cabinet and ministries in the form of cabinet resolutions or ministerial directives. These functions are mainly carried out by the Ministry of Promotion of Virtue and Prevention of Vice, which came into existence with the removal of the Ministry of Women's Affairs. The Taliban amir, a theocratic ruler who acts like a king, has appointed individuals who bear the titles of Akhund, Shaykh, Mufti and Mulavi, while it has dismissed the judiciary that existed under the erstwhile Republic.[12] The amir now has unlimited powers and executes laws at his will. He is the head of state who is the executive, legislative and the judiciary. He acts as the king used to under the 1964 Constitution.

The Taliban is believed to be coming out with a new constitution, but for that it would have to activate the Loya Jirga, or grand council, consisting of Afghan representatives appointed by provincial authorities and transitional government officials. Besides, as long as the Taliban runs an interim government, it will officially not be in a position to promulgate a constitution. The Taliban has not made any move to activate the Loya Jirga, because it is well aware that it has not created an inclusive government. Therefore, keeping the constitution aside – and it has become as good as invalid – the Taliban makes its own laws, dealing with crimes on the spot and giving verdicts through its own kangaroo courts. The Taliban of today knows too well that unlike during its previous tenure of 1996–2001, when Afghanistan had no political order, this is a changed country now, with not just a constitution in place but also knowledge of legal tenets and deeper understanding of the law among the Afghan youth. The Taliban has said it will bring back the constitution that was in prevalence under the monarchy in 1964, during the era of King Mohammad Zahir Shah, 'for the interim period without any content that is in conflict with Islamic Sharia and the principles of the Islamic Emirate'. This will only make things worse. However, the Taliban has been in a fix since making this statement, because that constitution has certain provisions that granted women the right to vote, allowing them to have increased participation in Afghan politics.[13]

The Western countries and Afghanistan's neighbours, including India, have been pressing the Taliban government to have a more inclusive government by giving prominent positions to people from the

EPILOGUE

minority Hazara communities. It has been threatened with isolation, stiff sanctions and stoppage of aid, but the Taliban has not relented. Even though it has expanded the cabinet, the Taliban has refused to have any women's representation in the government, making it more difficult for itself to gain international legitimacy. Without any positive and clear signs that the Taliban is willing to work towards a more inclusive governance model, international donors continue to be wary of lending support to a regime in the early stages of what remains an uncertain transition from militancy to government.[14]

To Recognise or Not to Recognise the Taliban

After two years of chaotic rule by the Taliban, during which hundreds and thousands have migrated out of the country for greener pastures, there is apprehension across the globe that Afghanistan might once again become a safe haven for terrorists. Asfandyar Mir, a senior expert on South Asia at the US Institute of Peace (USIP), points out that terrorist groups in Afghanistan fall into two categories. The first consists of allies of the Taliban, like the Al-Qaeda, the Tehreek-e-Taliban Pakistan (TTP) and the Central Asian jihadi units. The second consists of those opposed to the Taliban, primary among them being the Islamic State Khorasan (ISIS-K).[15] On 31 July 2022, in a development that shook the world, Ayman al-Zawahiri, then Al-Qaeda chief, was dramatically killed at his residence in central Kabul in a drone strike, which, incidentally, also told the world that America's counterterrorism strategy would continue to be active in that country. In other words, Afghanistan is not really free from 'foreigners'.

Zawahiri's family had moved to a safe house in Kabul in early 2022, several months after the Taliban takeover. As part of the agreement reached with the US in 2020, the Taliban had pledged not to provide shelter to Al-Qaeda. But the Taliban was aware of Zawahiri's presence in the country, according to US officials. The home he was staying in was reportedly owned by an aide to senior Taliban leader Sirajuddin Haqqani. It was located in Sherpur, a neighbourhood that had hosted Western embassies and wealthy residents for years. Following the US's counterterrorism operation – one may recall that the Al-Qaeda leader Osama bin Laden in 2011 was also killed in a special US Navy SEAL operation – US Secretary of State Anthony Blinken blamed the Taliban: 'The Taliban] grossly violated the Doha Agreement and repeated assurances to the world that they would not allow Afghan territory to be used by terrorists to threaten the security of other countries . . . They also betrayed the Afghan people and their own stated desire for recognition from and normalization with the international community.'

At 6.18 a.m. on 31 July, a CIA drone launched two Hellfire missiles at Zawahiri while he was standing on the balcony of his house. His family members were in other parts of the safe house at the time, so no one else

EPILOGUE

153

was injured in the precision strike, according to the US government. 'Zawahiri's death deals a significant blow to Al-Qaeda and will degrade the group's ability to operate, including against the US Homeland,' a senior White House official told reporters on 1 August.[16]

Despite all these, the Taliban has received indirect support from China, Pakistan, Turkey, Germany, Norway, the UAE, Saudi Arabia, Malaysia, Indonesia and Japan. Some countries, such as India, have reopened their embassies in Kabul but have not allowed the Taliban diplomats to officially take up roles in their own countries. Taliban diplomats continue to work clandestinely in some countries in the visa and political sections of the Afghan embassies. The Taliban has also maintained regular communication with all Afghan missions across the world, which includes those that continue to operate under the former tricolour flag representing the Republic. In New Delhi's posh Chanakyapuri area, where the Embassy of Afghanistan is located, framed life-sized photos of the former president Ghani continue to hang on the walls while the tricolour flies aloft in the main courtyard. While the embassy was operating smoothly, albeit with some financial difficulties till January–February 2023, tensions and infighting among diplomats who were posted here by the Ghani government engulfed its operations. More than half of the staff have left their jobs and settled in Canada, Belgium, the UK and the US. The embassy recently got embroiled in a major controversy when one of its former commercial counsellors claimed that he had been appointed as the new chargé d'affaires, as per a communication from Afghanistan's Ministry of Foreign Affairs, at a time when the previous ambassador, Farid Mamundzay, was on leave to meet his family settled in Europe. Mamundzay, who had been running the embassy with the paltry resources provided by the Indian government, sought India's intervention in the matter, but New Delhi stayed out of it, calling the development Afghanistan's 'internal matter'. But there is continued suspicion as to whether the Taliban has indeed settled inside the premises of the Afghan embassy in India.[17] Eventually, as 2023 came to a close, Mamundzay and his aides left India, handing over the embassy to India's Ministry of External Affairs. The embassy is currently being run by the two consul generals, posted in Mumbai and Hyderabad, to look after the needs of Afghans living in India or travelling within the country.[18] However, for daily operations of the embassy the diplomats deal with the Taliban as they are in power. Therefore, India, like other countries, is also dealing with the Taliban indirectly.

In complete contrast to its previous rule, when the Taliban unleashed an atmosphere of terror and fear, replete with mass murders and public executions, this time it has been making use of its sharp and shrewd diplomatic skills in dealing with the stakeholders. When it was in power previously, Saudi Arabia, Pakistan and the UAE had given the Taliban official recognition. But this time it has not been given that recognition. Still,

EPILOGUE

senior officials of the Taliban government continue to roam around the globe attending conferences, while many countries' special representatives for Afghanistan continue to hold meetings with the Taliban in Kabul. For many key countries, like China, it is business as usual when it comes to Afghanistan.

In other words, despite not being recognised de jure, the Taliban has been recognised de facto. Its Islamic Emirate has been steadily acknowledged. Of the 440 engagements, 153 (35 per cent) were with Middle Eastern states – the highest proportion of any regional bloc. Moreover, Western engagement with the Taliban has generally taken place at multilateral events, while states from other regions have favoured bilateral meetings. This trend highlights the continuing Western discomfort with the group. The West has restricted its interaction with the Taliban to international forums focused primarily on humanitarian aid.

However, the country that has engaged the most with the Taliban since it came to power is China, which is firm on its objective to alter the geopolitics of the Hindu Kush region. The Chinese foreign minister Wang Yi has met his Taliban counterpart Amir Khan Muttaqi several times in an effort to tap Afghanistan's vast and rich mineral and oil reserves while also promoting Chinese President Xi Jinping's pet project, the Belt and Road Initiative (BRI). The foreign ministry of China had said in 2022, during the first anniversary of Taliban rule in Afghanistan, that under the Islamist group the country was making a 'critical transition from chaos to order' even though the rulers face 'multiple challenges from within and outside that need to be addressed with more support and help'.

Russia too has increased its economic engagement with the Taliban. Both Beijing and Moscow have decided to do business with the new dispensation in Kabul so as to not isolate the Taliban. When Wang Yi visited Kabul in 2022, he met Interim Deputy Prime Minister Abdul Ghani Baradar and proposed an extension of the China–Pakistan Economic Corridor (CPEC) into Afghanistan, which would be developed as a 'bridge for regional connectivity'. In return for the promises to invest in Afghanistan, Wang Yi also had the Taliban cough up assurances that it would 'resolutely crack down on all terrorist forces, including the ETIM'. The ETIM, which is a UN-sanctioned terrorist organisation for its links with Al-Qaeda, Osama bin Laden and the Taliban, was established by militant Uighurs – a Turkic-speaking ethnic majority based in northwest China's Xinjiang province. The ETIM seeks to create an independent country by including parts of Turkey, Kazakhstan, Kyrgyzstan, Uzbekistan, Pakistan, Afghanistan, and the Xinjiang Uighur Autonomous Region (XUAR). The UN sanctioned ETIM on 11 September 2002 for 'participating in the financing, planning, facilitating, preparing or perpetrating of acts or activities by, in conjunction with, under the name of, on behalf or in support of'. China also made the clever move of entering Afghanistan at a time when the US and the European countries were bogged down with the Russia–Ukraine war and the Israel–Hamas conflict.

EPILOGUE

Meanwhile, due to the ongoing Russia–Ukraine war, which began in February 2022, the Moscow format of talks with the Taliban, which was launched in 2017, has slowed down. The Moscow format of talks is aimed at bringing all the stakeholders – India, Iran, China and Pakistan – in stitching up a political reconciliation between the Afghans who want to have a democratic set-up in the country and the Taliban. However, it appears that the bonhomie between the Taliban and the Russians has taken a backseat after the initial rounds of talks, as Moscow realised that the new Kabul government is just not ready to listen to its demands for the creation of an inclusive government and the reinstatement of the rights of women to obtain education and to pursue a career. Every initiative to bring security and stability to Afghanistan has failed and the country continues to remain an open challenge for the world. As a former Indian ambassador to Afghanistan puts it, 'What [can one] really say about the Taliban and Afghanistan? It is so jaded and no one has any answer to the problems there.'

However, this particular attitude towards Afghanistan has given the Taliban more leeway to continue to function as it pleases and not adhere to the international obligations laid out for it under the Doha Accord. It is crucial for Afghanistan's neighbours to engage with the Taliban, even if it comes at the cost of alienating their old allies from the Republic or the NRF. While both government officials of the former Republic and the NRF are justified in their calls and demands asking other countries not to engage with the Taliban, they also need to view the developments from other countries' perspective. Having a country like Afghanistan in one's immediate neighbourhood is not really a geopolitical dream for countries. It is immensely challenging for countries like India or China to control and restrain the fallout from a war in Afghanistan and also to put in place the necessary counterterrorism mechanisms. Their populations are huge and under constant threat of terrorist attacks. On 12 September 2023, in his address to the Stimson Centre, Thomas West, US special representative to Afghanistan, even admitted to Americans remaining in 'regular touch' with the Taliban in Doha.

The US controls an Afghan Affairs Unit to ensure that the intra-Afghan dialogue remains active so that an inclusive government can be formed by the Taliban. On terrorism in Afghanistan, West said, 'First, the Taliban need to fundamentally fulfil their security obligations.' He also highlighted the fact that while Al-Qaeda had been reduced to a 'historical nadir' since it moved to Afghanistan from Sudan in 1996, concerns still persist within America's security apparatus about other terror groups still operating from inside Afghanistan.[19] West's speech made it clear that the US still remains deeply engaged with the Taliban even as it continues to refer to the Doha agreement again and again as its only template to deal with the outfit, making it clear to other stakeholders that engaging the Taliban is critical.

EPILOGUE

Taliban or No Taliban, China Signals Continuity in Afghanistan

On 13 September 2022, China did what was inevitable – it became the first country to formally appoint a new ambassador to Afghanistan when the tenure of the previous envoy came to an end a little after the Taliban takeover. Beijing attempted to portray it as a routine diplomatic rotation, giving out a larger message to the world, particularly to the neighbouring countries, that it has recognised the Taliban government in Kabul as a natural progression in the politics of the landlocked country. The move, which became headline news, also showcases the fact that for China, the continuation of its bilateral ties with Afghanistan and keeping relations with it business-as-usual was important. China has maintained that it will continue with all its projects and investments there. Afghanistan remains a pivotal zone for the success of China's BRI. In 2022, just as the second year of Taliban rule in Afghanistan began, China, Pakistan and Afghanistan got together vowing to extend the flagship project under the BRI – the CPEC – into Afghanistan, giving it a prominent role in the ambitious initiative.

This decision stemmed from an MoU on the BRI project that was signed in 2016 between Beijing and Kabul during the time of the former Afghan government when Afghanistan decided to be part of the BRI. The MoU was signed in the presence of Afghanistan's former chief executive Abdullah Abdullah and China's prime minister at the time, Li Keqiang. While a lot has changed since then, not just in Afghanistan but also in China, Beijing has ensured the plan's continuity. It then stands to reason why the Taliban was ecstatic when Xi said he would extend the CPEC into Afghanistan. For the Taliban, this meant two crucial things – legitimacy, which the West has denied it, and inflow of funds, which the West will never give directly. In 2017, China began engaging in peacekeeping efforts between Pakistan and Afghanistan, following the deterioration in relations between the two neighbours. They also agreed to establish a China–Afghanistan–Pakistan trilateral cooperation and held their first trilateral dialogue later that year. Since 2001, China has kept a relative distance in the matter of putting boots on the ground, in a major signal to the West, particularly the US. But the Chinese Communist Party has occasionally provided financial and military assistance to previous Afghan governments.

Chinese president Xi has given the BRI project both a political and economic connotation while cleverly using it as diplomatic leverage with countries that are not in the good books of the West. When it comes to Afghanistan, China has been carefully designing its strategy, making meaningful inroads and establishing itself as a long-term player, seemingly not bothered about political upheavals. After coming to power in 2013, President Xi started focusing on Afghanistan the very next year. And the focus has remained intact since then, even after the political landscape has undergone a sea change with the collapse of the Republic and the coming in of the Taliban. In the immediate aftermath of the Taliban takeover, while all the diplomatic missions in Kabul pulled their shutters down and hastily queued up to run out of the country, China continued its presence there while carrying on with its work.

The groundwork for the prompt decision to be the first to have a diplomatic presence in Afghanistan after its takeover by the Taliban had been laid down much earlier. Over the years, China has maintained direct communication with the Taliban and both sides have met on several occasions, bilaterally and internationally, underscoring China's warming ties with the Islamist group.[20] These were the steady steps which over the years culminated in Beijing sending a new envoy to that country in September 2023, making it clear to the world that China would not abandon the Taliban. For Beijing it was a step towards the 'continuation' of its ties with Afghanistan. At least six other countries – Qatar, Russia, Kazakhstan, Turkmenistan, Tajikistan and Uzbekistan – have also retained their ambassadors in Afghanistan. Wang Yi had also been advocating that the West should stop imposing sanctions on Afghanistan.

In August 2014, China and Afghanistan signed the programme of 'exchange notes granting zero-tariff treatment to the exports of some Afghan goods' to China. Since 2015, 97 per cent of goods originating from Afghanistan and exported to China have been enjoying zero-tariff entry. China renewed this commitment on 1 December 2022, granting zero-tariff treatment to 98 per cent of the products it imported from Afghanistan. However, Afghanistan imposes relatively high tariff rates on raw material imports. Afghanistan's main trading partners are its neighbours, and China is among its largest. In 2020, China grew to become the second-largest export destination for Afghan goods, after Pakistan. The annual growth rate in the value of Afghanistan's exports to China between 2016 and 2020 reached 105 per cent, according to the International Trade Centre (ITC). Boosting the Afghan economy, Afghanistan's exports to China have grown over the last twenty-five years at a yearly rate of 4.84 per cent, from US$16.6 million in 1995 to US$49.53 million in 2021.

The Taliban has been in talks with China to reopen the historical Silk Road trade routes, particularly through the Wakhan Corridor. The Taliban government, or the Islamic Emirate of Afghanistan (IEA), has already begun work on opening this corridor, in an effort to transform it into a reliable route for the transit of goods. The IEA is well aware that under the current conditions, the Wakhan Corridor project will aid in the rebuilding of Afghanistan and in its transition into a country that produces goods that are in demand all over the world. However, the construction of the Wakhan Corridor route will cost billions of dollars.[21]

China's strategy in Afghanistan is guided by its economic and security interests in that country. However, Beijing is also concerned about possible terror threats emanating from that country, which can have a direct bearing on China's national security concerns, particularly at a time when Beijing faces backlash from countries around the world and tensions between the US and China are soaring, on issues ranging from technology to Taiwan. As far as Afghanistan is concerned, China's primary concerns are regional instability and the potential for it to become a safe haven for terrorist groups, such as Uighur militants. China is closely monitoring the Taliban's relationship with the ETIM, as discussed earlier in the book. ETIM is a Muslim separatist group founded by militant Uighurs, members of the Turkic-speaking ethnic majority in the northwestern Chinese province of Xinjiang, which shares its borders with Afghanistan, Pakistan and six other countries.

China was also the first country to help Afghanistan with humanitarian aid – worth US$31 million – post the withdrawal of US troops from that country in August 2021. The Taliban regime, which had been facing a humanitarian catastrophe and economic meltdown, welcomed Beijing's prompt delivery of food and medical supplies, and that set the stage for the deepening of political and economic ties between the two sides. In March 2022, Chinese Foreign Minister Wang Yi made a stopover in Afghanistan before visiting India and held a meeting with the Taliban foreign minister, Amir Khan Muttaqi. Muttaqi told him that Afghanistan is willing to be a bridge for regional connectivity and a place of happiness and prosperity for its people rather than a source of war and turbulence; that Afghanistan is ready to actively participate in the BRI project and strengthen trade and investment cooperation with China; that it is willing to deepen friendly exchanges with neighbouring countries and jointly safeguard regional peace and stability.[22] Beijing also invited the Taliban to participate in the Third Foreign Ministers' Meeting among the neighbouring countries of Afghanistan, held in the city of Tunxi on 3 March 2022. It was the first time a Taliban official had attended this gathering, which involved China, Iran, Pakistan, Russia, Tajikistan, Turkmenistan and Uzbekistan. India, for obvious reasons, was not invited to this meet.

The first chapter of this dialogue was hosted in Islamabad in September 2021, immediately after the Taliban had seized power in Afghanistan. Iran had hosted the second meeting in late October, in Tehran. China's economic interests in Afghanistan revolve around significant investments in the mining sector – in the Mes Aynak copper mine and the oil extraction contract in respect of the northern provinces of Farvab and Sar-e-Pol. Both these projects were on hold due to the war and the smaller skirmishes, bomb blasts and terrorism there. However, post August 2021, Chinese mining companies have turned up in Afghanistan in hordes, eager to forge a deal with the Taliban.[23]

Assuming charge of the Chinese embassy in Kabul in September 2023, Beijing's newly appointed envoy, Zhao Sheng, highlighted China's policy of 'Three Respects' and 'Three Nevers' in dealing with Afghanistan. The 'Three Respects' are – China respects the independence, sovereignty and territorial integrity of Afghanistan, the independent choices made by the Afghan people, and the religious beliefs and national customs of Afghanistan. The 'Three Nevers' are – China never interferes

EPILOGUE

in Afghanistan's internal affairs, never seeks selfish interests in Afghanistan and never pursues the so-called 'sphere of influence'. In his first message to Afghanistan, the ambassador said:

> Amity and good neighborliness are invaluable to a country . . . The Chinese Embassy is committed to deepening practical cooperation in various fields under the framework of the Belt and Road Initiative, and promoting the sustained, healthy and steady development of China–Afghanistan relations. We will continue to deepen the traditional friendship between our two peoples, and share more fruits of China's development with Afghanistan. It is my belief that with our joint efforts, the towering tree of China–Afghanistan community with a shared future that features peace, development, openness, inclusiveness and solidarity will surely grow taller and stronger in the future![24]

Taliban's Complex Relationship with Pakistan and the TTP

The escalating tensions that we see today between Pakistan and Afghanistan over the TTP, also called Pakistan Taliban, are also a creation of the British and relate to the border the British drew between them when Pakistan was part of northwestern India.

The TTP was founded in 2007 following the US invasion of Afghanistan in 2001 in the aftermath of the 9/11 attacks. It is among the deadliest terrorist outfits in Pakistan. The group turned against the state of Pakistan for supporting America's 'War on Terror' and began sheltering members of the Afghan Taliban and Al-Qaeda who were fleeing the war in Afghanistan. Ever since the Taliban came to power in Afghanistan, the TTP also started strategising in exerting its influence and control in Pakistan and implementing the Islamic law, or the Sharia law. Of late, the TTP's terrorist activities have intensified even as the peace negotiations by the former Imran Khan government of Pakistan failed. The former Pakistan prime minister Khan wanted to negotiate a peace settlement with the TTP after the Afghan Taliban came to power in Kabul.

The evolution of the northwestern border of British India was a protracted and cumbersome process, which also got the Maharaja of Kashmir involved in the matter of Chitral and Gilgit. Pursuing its forward policy since the days of the Great Game, the British drew up its borders on the northwest (Durand Line), north (Gilgit) and northeast (McMahon Line) frontiers. The Anglo-Russian agreement over the Pamirs in 1895 had settled the border between Russia and Afghanistan, while the Durand agreement of 1893 defined the border between Afghanistan and British India, which Afghanistan never accepted. The Anglo-Russian Convention of 1907 was to formally recognise Afghanistan as a buffer between the British and Russian empires in Asia so that it ceased to be a bone of contention between them. The settling of the limits of Afghanistan also resulted in the settling of the eastern limits of Russia's physical advance into the Pamirs, but this fact was not so clear in 1895 to several

EPILOGUE

British strategists brought up in the old tradition of the Great Game. The Durand Line runs through Pashtun villages and has been the cause of constant tension between Afghanistan and Pakistan. Due to continuous tensions both within and between the two countries, the Durand Line never got administered by either country's government, leaving the place vulnerable to continual tensions and attacks.

While the borders between Pakistan and Afghanistan have witnessed recurring clashes and conflicts, the coming back of the Taliban has compounded the problems. While initially, when the Taliban seized power, it seemed as if all tensions between Kabul and Islamabad had come to an end, the then Imran Khan government in Pakistan openly claimed that it was country that had brought the Taliban back and even got the Doha deal brokered between the fundamentalist group and the Americans. But the Taliban never accepted this.

Within days of the Taliban takeover, while the Afghans were frantically running to the airport to flee their country leaving behind their lives and homes, or hiding in their homes or getting killed, Pakistan's then chief of the ISI, Lt Gen. Faiz Hamid, had visited Kabul on 4 September 2021. The Abbey Gate tragedy had taken place just days before, on 26 August 2021, reportedly carried out by the ISIS-K. A photo of Hamid holding an espresso in the lobby of Kabul's Serena Hotel, chatting and laughing with the then Islamabad envoy to Kabul Mansoor Khan and his other colleagues, had gone viral. Hamid's body language was that of someone who had achieved victory. And as if he would next write Afghanistan's future, he announced, 'Everything will be all right', in what came to be widely derided as 'Serena swagger'. While the media around the world and many experts said it was a surprise visit by Hamid to Kabul, it was anything but that.

A senior Pakistani government official told me later that the visit had been planned much in advance as Pakistan wanted to bring Taliban leader Mullah Abdul Ghani Baradar, who had been hiding in Pakistan for several years before his arrest in 2010, into the glare of the global media. Baradar, co-founder of the Taliban, had gained prominence during the peace talks with the US. However, after the Taliban came to power in Kabul, Pakistan wanted to ensure that he got global acceptance as a prominent figure. Hamid and his bosses back home had thought that a Taliban regime in Afghanistan with personalities like Akhundzada, Baradar and others at the helm of affairs would settle their woes with respect to the TTP and also diminish India's presence and influence in the region. The Ghani government had a positive relationship with India, which had always upset Pakistan.

Besides, Rawalpindi, headquarters of the Pakistan Army, also thought the Taliban would bring the TTP to the negotiating table. But nothing of the sort happened. In fact, on the contrary, the TTP became more aggressive, bringing the Pakistan Army down on its knees. Evidently, Hamid was shown the door by his supremo and eventually the Imran Khan government

EPILOGUE   169

was also overthrown even as tensions between the TTP and the Pakistani forces spiralled out of control. On the other hand, the hope that Pakistan had in reducing India's influence in Afghanistan backfired as the Taliban openly announced that it wanted to have friendly ties with New Delhi, urging the Indian government to reopen its embassy and continue with the infrastructure work left incomplete post August 2021.

Tensions between Afghanistan and Pakistan have only increased since the Taliban came to power. The surge in attacks on the Pakistan Army by the TTP has weakened the army, which does not have the financial capacity to launch large-scale counter-attacks. On September 2023, at least four senior Pakistani soldiers and twelve armed fighters were killed in clashes near the Pakistan–Afghanistan border, with the TTP claiming responsibility. This incident had been preceded by many such clashes in which the Pakistani army had to suffer massive losses as the Taliban was now equipped and trained with American guns and ammunition. To add to this, the economic situation in Pakistan has not just broken the morale of the Pakistani army but has also denied them the latest equipment.

Founded in 2007, the TTP is ideologically aligned with the ruling Taliban in Afghanistan. It seeks stricter enforcement of Islamic laws in Pakistan, the release of its members in government custody and a reduced Pakistani military presence in parts of Khyber Pakhtunkhwa, where it is running a shadow government.[25] TTP leaders also publicly say that the group seeks to establish an Islamic caliphate in Pakistan, which would require the overthrow of the Pakistani government. The TTP has also historically maintained close ties with senior Al-Qaeda leaders, including Al-Qaeda's former head of operations for Pakistan.

Baitullah Mehsud, the first TTP leader, died on 5 August 2009, and his successor, Hakimullah Mehsud, died on 1 November 2013. TTP's central shura in November 2013 appointed Mullah Fazlullah as the group's overall leader. A shura, or council, is a quintessential body dealing with local village-level politics in Afghanistan. These bodies often act as liaison agencies between the local political leaders and the central government. Most prominent among these shuras is the Quetta Shura which is the nerve centre of all Taliban leaders. The Quetta Shura has been instrumental in planning, designing and executing multi-pronged insurgency movements in Pakistan's Balochistan Province.

Fazlullah is staunchly anti-Western, anti-Islamabad, and advocates harsh tactics, underscored by his ordering of the November 2012 attempted assassination of education rights activist Malala Yousafzai. Since 2008, the TTP has repeatedly and publicly threatened to attack the US homeland. A TTP spokesman claimed responsibility for the failed vehicle-bomb attack in Times Square, New York City, on 1 May 2010. In June 2011, a spokesman vowed to attack the US and Europe in revenge for the death of Osama bin Laden. A TTP leader in April 2012 endorsed external operations by the group and threatened attacks in the UK for its involvement

EPILOGUE

in Afghanistan.[26] Also known as the Pakistani Taliban, this group has shown a resurrection of sorts after the Taliban's victory in Afghanistan. The TTP has been able to strengthen its ranks substantially by merging other smaller splinter groups into itself, thereby widening its base and increasing the frequency of its operations.

The victory of the Taliban in Afghanistan has also given the TTP a psychological boost while exposing the weaknesses of the Pakistani military and its capacity to confront multiple challenges. The TTP has also been able to rise up the ladder because of the weak responses it has observed on the part of the Pakistani army. The TTP, Pakistani sources tell me, is now well-positioned to chalk out a strategy to gain control over Pakistan, like their Afghan brethren, while closing all roads to an amicable solution and a political settlement with the Pakistan government. It is believed to be arming itself heavily and also coming down heavily on the Pakistani military, and its bosses are believed to be hatching a plan to take advantage of the current political situation in Pakistan, where the civil–military relationship is witnessing unprecedented threats to its existence and the political scene remains volatile.

When the Taliban returned to power, the TTP claimed that it was a great victory for its jihadi project. In an ideological alignment of sorts with the Taliban, Mufti Noor Wali Mehsud, the fourth amir of the TTP, made it public that his group would owe its allegiance to the amir of the Taliban, Hibatullah Akhundzada, and vowed lifelong support to the Afghan Taliban. Mehsud, on the other hand, proclaimed that after fighting the US and the allied forces in Afghanistan side-by-side with the Afghan Taliban, the TTP would now work towards bringing stability to the Taliban regime, ensuring that it survived in the country and would not be overthrown by foreign fighters again.

Yet another factor that has induced new vigour into the rank and file of the TTP has been the freeing of many of its fighters who had been lodged in various prisons across Afghanistan by the American forces. They included senior commanders like the TTP's founding deputy amir, Maulvi Faqir Muhammad Bajauri, who was imprisoned in 2013, and former spokesperson Mufti Khalid Balti, who was jailed in 2015. As soon as he was freed, Bajauri started giving directions and sermons to TTP fighters, exhorting them to take the Pakistani military head-on. He also claimed that the TTP would achieve the same kind of victory as the Afghan Taliban had in Afghanistan. But interestingly, the Afghan Taliban has never publicly declared any conflict with Pakistan even though it supports the TTP purely on an ideological basis. But the Taliban foot soldiers harbour a deep sense of dislike for Pakistan.[27]

The Taliban's senior leadership is now also making an effort towards to ensure that it is not seen by the world as a bunch of Islamabad's lackeys as it fights hard to gain international recognition. The simmering tensions between the two neighbours came out into the open when, during the 2022 Asia Cup cricket match held in September 2022 in Sharjah, Afghan fans threw chairs and other items at Pakistani fans in the stadium after their team lost. The

EPILOGUE 173

stadium resonated with sloganeering from both sides as Pakistanis called Afghans 'terrorists' and the Afghans called the Pakistanis 'traitors'. Thereafter, in December 2022, an assassination attempt was made in Kabul on the head of the Pakistani mission in Afghanistan, Ubaid Ur Rehman Nizamani, which further impacted the bilateral ties between the two countries, creating deep divisions even within their political class.[28]

The root cause of the Taliban movement in Afghanistan and Pakistan was the rise of Pashtun nationalism. It was the Pashtun tribes that gave shape to the kingdom of Afghanistan, and that is the reason why the rural Pashtun population accepted Taliban rule in the 1990s rather willingly. In the traditional Pashtun governance culture, the role of the state is limited and the will of God is supreme. Pashtuns have historically opposed three forms of government – those lacking traditional or religious ideology or legitimacy, those that impose a plethora of taxes on the common man, and those that attempt to alter their lives, their socioeconomic norms and way of life.

Pakistan itself has been going through a severe upheaval in its domestic politics ever since the Taliban returned to Kabul. The Imran Khan government, which was believed to have aided and abetted the comeback of the Taliban in Afghanistan, has since been overthrown. The former-cricketer-turned-prime-minister is himself battling several charges of corruption. The Shahbaz Sharif government which succeeded him also melted away by 2023. Pakistan came under a caretaker government led by interim prime minister Anwaar-ul-Haq Kakar.

THE FALL OF KABUL

When Kakar visited New York in September 2023 to attend the UN General Assembly meetings, he sought to portray one-upmanship over Afghanistan. During his visit to Washington he addressed the Council on Foreign Relations (CFR), where he spoke at length on the situation between the TTP and the Afghan Taliban. He said, 'A stable Afghanistan continues to remain an important foreign policy priority for Pakistan and the US. We welcome the US direct engagement with the Afghan government, and on our part would continue to push them to honour their commitment to women's rights, girls' education, and ensuring the Afghan soil is not used for terrorist attacks against other countries.'

The caretaker prime minister of Pakistan also said:

It is in the interest of the de facto Afghan government also that such entities who are violent, who would challenge their own rationale even of taking over a forceful government but still claim that they can monopolise the violence in the given territory, if that idea is basically challenged by any group, it doesn't look good on their part [Kakar was taking a jibe at the Taliban government in Afghanistan]. So there is, in some areas, convergence of interest that those groups should be curtailed, controlled, managed as far as their violent capacity is concerned . . . My soldiers are being killed on a daily basis. The civilian populace is being targeted on a daily basis, particularly in the two provinces of Balochistan and Khyber Pakhtunkhwa. We have to set the milestones which are achievable, which are doable. And we do believe that we are not alone in resolving this issue, because the threat at a level

EPILOGUE   175

it is imminent for Pakistan, but in the midterm future
I feel it is a threat to the whole region. So a regional
approach is required, along with all the neighbourhood
of Afghanistan.

On 8 February, elections were held across Pakistan, and
demolishing all pre-poll predictions that ex-PM Nawaz
Sharif will have a clean sweep, it was Imran Khan's
Pakistan Tehreek-e-Insaf (PTI) and its independent
candidates that outdid everyone. By the time their election
commission declared the results on 11 February, the state
of Pakistan was still undecided as to who will become
their prime minister and as of writing this, none of the
three major parties of that country – Pakistan Muslim
League Nawaz party (PML-N), Pakistan People's Party
(PPP) and PTI – could win the required 169 seats to
have a majority in parliament. But in all probability it
appeared to be a comeback for Sharif.

The Afghan Economy After the Taliban Takeover

The Afghan economy collapsed completely after the
disintegration of the Ashraf Ghani government and
the Taliban's comeback. An average middle-class or
lower-middle-class Afghan today, and that too in a
well-off city like Kabul, is much poorer and hungrier
than when the previous government was in power. The
Afghan economy suffered multiple shocks after the
Taliban takeover. Natural disasters such as droughts
and floods ravaged several provinces and rural areas.

Like other countries, Afghanistan too suffered the adverse impacts of the COVID-19 pandemic. On top of all this were the biting US and UN sanctions, the freezing of Afghanistan's foreign exchange reserves of $9 billion by the Biden administration and the foreign banks' reluctance to do business with the country. In 2021, the Afghan economy, as measured by gross domestic product (GDP), fell 20–30 per cent year on year, according to the United Nations Development Program and the International Monetary Fund.[29]

As the Taliban men came riding into the heart of the Afghan capital in their pickup trucks, waving their white flags, foreign aid amounting to $8 billion per year came to an abrupt end, leading to a collapse in public spending and dealing a blow to the Afghan economy.

According to the World Bank, job losses and economic deprivation were widespread and the GDP contracted by 20.7 per cent in 2021. As aid to Afghanistan was partially resumed (off-budget and on a smaller scale – about US$3.5 billion, against US$9 billion in 2020), signs emerged by mid-2022 that the Afghan economy was settling at a fragile, low-level equilibrium. Yet these signs of stabilisation could not lift the substantial pressures Afghan families faced in sustaining their livelihoods, as a contraction of aid-driven services and security sectors spilled over into other sectors of the economy, affecting welfare distribution across the chain. But the Afghan (AFN) preserved its value against the major currencies. The UN cash shipments for humanitarian and basic service support remained significant. They continued

EPILOGUE 177

to underlie currency stability – in February 2023 alone, US$240 million was shipped to Afghanistan through the UN and other international NGOs, making for a total support of US$440 million in January–February 2023 (against a cumulative US$1.85 billion in 2022, which amounted to about US$154 million monthly). By mid-2022, two-thirds of Afghan households reportedly could not afford food and other basic non-food items, forcing many adults to engage in low-productivity activities to generate income. In addition, living conditions during the harsh winter months worsened, partly because of significant electricity shortages in the cities. Low demand remains a critical constraint to the rebound of the private sector, the World Bank noted.[30]

After peaking in mid-2022, inflation has turned into deflation since April 2023, driven by the easing of supply constraints and wider availability of goods in the markets. About two-thirds of Afghan households face challenges in maintaining their livelihoods and consumption. Despite the country's widening merchandise trade deficit, the Afghan appreciated against major currencies from January to August 2023. There has been a shortfall in revenues against the targets because of underperformance in inland revenue collections, stated the 'Afghanistan Economic Monitor' produced by the World Bank.[31]

During my visit to Afghanistan, it took me a while to fathom the poverty one saw on the roads of Kabul, and at the cost of repeating myself I have to mention again that on my first day there I was asked to report on the security situation and the mood in the country in the run-up to the withdrawal of the US troops, but I ended up reporting on the poverty there and how the people were not concerned about whether the Taliban was coming or not, whether Ghani stayed or left, whether the US troops but stayed back or withdrew, whether the intra-Afghan talks were on or off . . . they were busy procuring their bread for the day. I remember the day I had walked back to the Serena when my taxi got stuck in a jam, I saw a man walking with a boy, roughly six and perhaps his son, towards a bread shop. They stood near the window of the shop where bread was being distributed, wrapped in newspaper. There was a small queue, so they had to wait. They looked hungry but the boy stood silently with his father. When their turn came and the man in the shop brought out about five loaves of bread, loosely tied them up in a newspaper and handed them over, their eyes were shining and their faces broke into wide smiles. Both sat on the pavement there itself and began to eat. I could not take a photo of them, but that particular sight remains etched in my mind.

Roughly 15 million people go to sleep hungry every night in Afghanistan, UN's World Food Programme says. However, according to the programme's rough estimates, US$1 billion is what it will take to pull millions of families back from the brink of starvation ahead of the harsh, unforgiving Afghan winter. In 2023, the WFP in Afghanistan was forced to stop life-saving assistance for 10 million people, deepening despair and worry for Afghans. Due to a massive

EPILOGUE 179

funding shortfall, the WFP will now only be able to provide emergency assistance to 3 million people per month. The WFP has been appealing to donor governments to prioritise the funding of humanitarian operations in Afghanistan. The organisation is in the midst of a crippling funds crisis, which is forcing it to scale back life-saving assistance at a time when acute hunger is at record levels. Almost half of WFP country operations have already cut – or plan to cut soon - the size and scope of their food, cash and nutrition assistance programmes.[32]

The America Story Is Not Over Yet in Afghanistan

Afghanistan will never be the same again, neither for the world nor for the Afghans, including the Taliban. The entry of the American soldiers and allied forces twenty-two years back has changed the country. The Afghans are no longer a population that lives in a primitive era cut off from the world, as was the situation in 1996 when the Taliban came to power there for the first time. Today, even the Taliban foreign minister and others in the government travel abroad on private jets holding files in their hands. The minister takes briefings from his team, as if he were a key world leader. While we may choose to sneer at this, for serious Afghanistan watchers this is a great shift from the earlier Taliban. This is a Taliban that speaks good English, that knows how to negotiate – and do note here that it is this Taliban that sat on the opposite side of the table facing the Americans and got the Doha deal signed to its advantage. It is based on this very agreement that the Taliban came back to power, defeating all the forces of the Republic as well as international troops by effectively leveraging the understanding reached in the Doha deal.

Therefore, today when the US speaks of the Taliban violating the Doha deal by refusing to allow girls and women to receive a formal education or to form an inclusive government, it is quite puzzling. Because by signing the Doha deal, which spoke of an Islamic Emirate, the US did indirectly recognise the Taliban. So, if today the US is saying something different, it is just trying to obfuscate the truth of what happened during the withdrawal.

In an interview with ABC News on the second anniversary of the US withdrawal from Afghanistan, General Mark Milley, chairman of the United States Joint Chiefs of Staff, who retired in September 2023, said the war 'didn't end the way I wanted'. He said:

> In the broader sense, the war was lost. We were fighting the Taliban and their allies for 20-plus years. And they prevailed in that capital for a lot of reasons . . . But, sure, lots of regrets by a lot of us from, from 9/11 on . . . when the enemy is occupying your capital . . . that's a strategic setback, strategic failure. That's what I testified to in public. And there's no way you can describe that as a strategic success.[33]

In September 2021, General Milley was subjected to a six-hour-long public testimony for the chaotic

EPILOGUE

withdrawal, the enormous evacuation process and the American drone strike that killed ten Afghans, including seven children, in Kabul on 29 August 2021. During that testimony, General Milley admitted to having recommended to President Biden that a minimum of 2,500 American troops be kept back in Afghanistan while the evacuation and withdrawal took place.

During the same testimony, the US Secretary of Defence Lloyd Austin said the collapse of the Afghan Army during the final months of the war took everyone by surprise. Referring to the previous Ghani government, Austin said:

> We need to consider some uncomfortable truths: that we did not fully comprehend the depth of corruption and poor leadership in their senior ranks, that we didn't grasp the damaging effect of frequent and unexplained rotations by President Ghani of his commanders, that we did not anticipate the snowball effect caused by the deals that the Taliban commanders struck with local leaders ... We failed to fully grasp that there was only so much for which – and for whom – many of the Afghan forces would fight.[34]

The US Congress also set up an 'Afghanistan War Commission' in December 2021 in order to conduct a comprehensive review of key decisions related to US military, intelligence, foreign assistance and diplomatic involvement in Afghanistan from June 2001 to August 2021. This was established under Section 1094 of the National Defense Authorization Act for fiscal year 2022

(Public Law 117-81). Linda Robinson, a journalist and author who has covered Afghanistan extensively, wrote in a report published by the US-based CFR:

> However dramatic it appeared, the collapse of the Afghan government and military was not surprising. The seeds of defeat were planted long before President Joe Biden ordered the withdrawal. His predecessor, Donald Trump, signed an accord with the Taliban in February 2020 that set a 2021 withdrawal date and decoupled the US departure from any agreement to end the fighting among Afghans – thereby ceding the primary source of leverage. Afghan morale plummeted. Negotiations to reach a political settlement were never the central priority at any point in the war, as ephemeral military targets or 'conditions' substituted for hardheaded recognition that there were in essence two Afghanistans, and that the Taliban always controlled most of the rural one (where I spent most of my time). Compounding this error, the US government sought to implement centralized models of governance and military institutions that were inappropriate, imperfectly realized, and expensive to sustain. Finally, the US and its allies set aspirational goals for societal transformation that could not be achieved on a relatively slim support base of urbanized, educated Afghans . . . In sum, the American project was not based in a clear understanding of the realities of Afghanistan. Well-meaning Americans believed that they could persuade, cajole, or force a project that much of the population did not actively embrace or participate in. A chain of discrete policy errors flowed from this basic failure to adequately understand the country. Several fundamental lessons emerge from scrutinizing

EPILOGUE 183

these errors in the design and execution of political, diplomatic, military, and economic policies.[35] The images of Afghans, especially of the youth, clinging to running planes, of parents trying to climb the wall of the airport to hand over their children, even newborns, across barbed wire fences, of the Taliban taking over the entire capital city, shook the world even as America's strategic failure stood exposed, just as it did during the Vietnam war. The US, however, continued to safeguard its own interests, which can be seen in the killing of al-Zawahiri and its eventual release of a $450 million package to Pakistan Air Force for maintenance of its F-16 fighter fleet. Apparently, it was Islamabad that provided the intelligence inputs on Zawahiri's whereabouts to Washington, informing it that he was in a safe house in Kabul sheltered by the Taliban.

Coming to the Afghan War Commission, which was created by the US Congress on December 2021, it claims to be bipartisan, aiming to minutely scrutinise each and every decision taken by the US government in Afghanistan since it first entered the country in 2001 till the day it withdrew in 2021. According to the commission's co-chairs, Shamila N. Chaudhary and Colin F. Jackson, the body has been entrusted with three broad tasks:

First, it must write an official history of the engagement, studying the decisions made and their consequences, presenting it in a manner accessible to both expert and general audiences. Second, it aims to derive foresight from hindsight, extracting the lessons learned from this

20-year project. Identifying insights that can be applied to future interventions in different contexts presents a more formidable challenge. Third, and most difficult, is the call for recommendations, identifying changes in government structure and processes that can enhance US performance in future interventions and avoid the pitfalls we encountered in Afghanistan.[36]

The US withdrawal from Afghanistan was not only chaotic but also deadly. Just as American troops and their allies were in the final wind-up mode, a deafening blast ripped through the thick crowd that had assembled outside the technical section of Kabul airport near Abbey Gate, killing around 200 Afghans and 13 American soldiers. According to the Pentagon, the dastardly act was carried out by the ISIS. America's leading broadcaster CNN carried out an investigation on what exactly happened during the Abbey Gate incident, questioning whether it was only due to the blast that so many people got killed or whether they were shot. Many victims of that blast whom CNN met as part of the investigation said they saw '[US] soldiers firing on those who were standing' there that day. One of them said the 'shooting seemed to start straight after the explosion'. A doctor from the Wazir Akbar Khan Hospital also said he received several injured who had gunshots on their bodies.[37]

While these investigations will keep taking place, and some may or may not reach a logical end that answers all the questions, the reality is that Afghanistan is now back in the hands of the Taliban. US Presidents Donald Trump, Joe Biden – and in my opinion Barack Obama

EPILOGUE 185

too, to some extent – are responsible for how the war ended and where it has brought Afghanistan, pushing it back to the dark ages where women do not even have the basic dignity of life. While it is a hard fact of life that women all around the world have to fight a tough battle, whether inside their homes or outside, life is certainly way too difficult, harsh and rude for Afghan women living in Afghanistan. The policies adopted by each of the three US Presidents mentioned above led to the eventual collapse of the Republic and the Afghan National Defense and Security Forces (ANDSF). The ANDSF was never made self-sustainable and self-dependent, despite a whopping $90 billion being spent on supporting it for over two decades.

Importantly, it was the final collapse of the ANDSF that opened the gates for the Taliban to walk freely into the Afghan capital. The country in which the US and NATO had spent two decades fighting Al-Qaeda and the Taliban came under the control of the same Taliban that the US had deposed after 9/11. Ironically, the Taliban did not have to fire a single shot or kill even one person to enter the capital where it had once ruled.

When the US under President Obama made the first announcement in June 2011 that America was now going to wrap up its long-drawn adventure in Afghanistan and would gradually embark on a drawdown exercise, the Afghan government should have immediately started taking effective measures to keep the governance ecosystem robust and stable and the ANDSF a professional armed force.

Addressing the American people on the way forward in Afghanistan in the aftermath of Osama bin Laden's death, Obama stated that the US, with its NATO allies, had made substantial progress on the objectives it had in mind when it entered Afghanistan. He said the US had ensured that it put Al-Qaeda on the 'path to defeat' and would 'not relent until the job is done'. Obama boasted that the American forces had 'inflicted serious losses on the Taliban and taken a number of its strongholds'.

He said, 'We do know that peace cannot come to a land that has known so much war without a political settlement. So as we strengthen the Afghan government and security forces, America will join initiatives that reconcile the Afghan people, including the Taliban.'[38]

But neither the former Afghan president Hamid Karzai nor his successor Ashraf Ghani were able to fulfil the objectives of securing Afghanistan's future, bringing in peace and developing a credible national security strategy. The Ghani government proved to be morally corrupt and was solely responsible for driving the final nail in the coffin of the Republic. The Ghani government treated the ANDSF like its personal security guard force. The administration used to randomly shuffle around senior commanders in the force and appoint its own loyalists, mostly on the basis of their ethnicity, which brought politics and discrimination into the Afghan armed forces. This proved to be deadly, for the forces started to break from within as a result of the weakened chains of command and morale, which ultimately killed the

EPILOGUE

spirit of the soldiers to fight for their country. The young and dynamic Afghan soldiers, who were trained by the US and NATO forces, increasingly began to feel marginalised and their connection with the US was seen as a liability by Washington. The Taliban took advantage of each of these weaknesses that slowly crept into the ANDSF. Besides, the Taliban's media and psychological warfare campaign, magnified by real-time reporting, further undermined the Afghan forces' determination to fight.[39]

The Taliban leveraged every possible issue that the officers in the ANDSF faced and turned each into an advantage. It began to negotiate with those soldiers who were marginalised within their own ranks or were seen as a liability or were vulnerable, bringing them into their fold by offering them substantial amounts of money in monthly salary. In cases where this strategy failed, the Taliban would launch a direct assault on them. This went on for years and years, and that was how the Taliban tactfully won district after district, province after province. The ANSDF became prone to failure also because of the US forces' inability to set realistic objectives and goals for them, as Washington was driven by political motives and not by a genuine need to develop the force, a report by the Special Inspector General for Afghanistan Reconstruction (SIGAR) said.

SIGAR also found out from an investigation after the NATO troops' withdrawal that the US military was tasked with balancing competing requirements. For example, battlefield success for the ANSDF was critical to create the conditions necessary to draw down the US combat forces in Afghanistan. But because the US troops were far more effective at fighting, they often led missions or filled critical gaps in missions – providing close air support, airstrikes, medical evacuation, logistics and intelligence gathering – at the expense of the ANDSF gaining experience by fighting on its own. As a result, the ANDSF became overly reliant on borrowed capabilities.[40]

The US, if the American media is to be believed, thinks that the Taliban has all but 'extinguished' Al-Qaeda, Washington's enemy No. 1. In an editorial authored by David Ignatius of the *Washington Post*, who was able to access certain reports by the US intelligence on what seemed to be an 'obituary' of Al-Qaeda, the terror group's ability to launch an assault on America such as the 9/11 attack 'is at its lowest point' and 'only a small number of members [are] left in Afghanistan'.[41] During a meeting in July 2023 between the special representative for Afghanistan, Thomas West, special envoy for Afghan women, girls and human rights, Rina Amiri, chief of the US mission to Afghanistan based in Doha, Karen Decker, and senior Taliban representatives and technocrat-professionals in Doha, Qatar, the American delegation acknowledged that there had been a decrease in large-scale terrorist attacks against Afghan civilians. US officials pressed for the immediate and unconditional release of US citizens who had been detained by the Taliban, noting that these detentions were a significant obstacle to its positive engagement with Afghanistan.

EPILOGUE

189

The US State Department said in a statement that at the same meeting the US had taken note of reports indicating that the Taliban's ban on opium poppy cultivation had resulted in a significant decrease in cultivation during the most recent growing season. But the US officials registered serious concerns regarding the continuing trafficking and sale of processed opiates and synthetic drugs. The American delegation voiced its openness to continue the dialogue on countering the narcotics trade out of Afghanistan.[42]

However, today a bigger challenge has cropped up in Afghanistan, which can prove to be detrimental to the national security interests of not only its neighbours but also those who continue to treat the country as their favourite battlefield. This is the challenge of the ISIS-K, the group responsible for the blasts outside the Kabul airport in August 2021. The ISIS-K can be anybody. Its members do not have to necessarily wear traditional attire like the Taliban to spread terror, and they are far deadlier. Over the years, the group has changed its strategic objectives to remain relevant and to be able to spread massive terror across several geographies. Among the many ambitions the group harbours, one is to 'purify' Afghanistan by eliminating the Afghan Taliban as well as minority groups like the Hazaras.[43]

In order to achieve this objective, the ISIS-K took fighters from Pakistan's TTP and Al-Qaeda's foot soldiers from both Afghanistan and Pakistan. In order to assert its influence and gain large tracts of territory, the ISIS-K also tapped into the Salafis from the eastern part of Afghanistan, with the help of whom it could implement its hegemony over the provinces of Nangarhar and Kunar. Before the US withdrawal from Afghanistan, the group had been suffering a major setback from multiple attacks on it by the ANDSF, the US military and the Afghan Taliban, which weakened it from the inside. However, the group has been able to continue its operations by consistently regrouping under the leadership of Shahab al-Muhajir and has changed its modus operandi to target urban centres such as Kabul to garner the attention of the global media and thereby the international community. They are also active in all the countries that border Afghanistan, such as Uzbekistan, Tajikistan and Iran.[44]

Muhajir, aka Sanaullah Ghafari, the ISIS-K's current amir, was appointed by the ISIS core to lead the ISIS-K in June 2020. Ghafari is responsible for approving all ISIS-K operations throughout Afghanistan and arranging funds for them. He, along with Sultan Aziz Azam, spokesperson of the ISIS-K, and Maulawi Rajab, also known as Maulawi Rajab Salahudin, a senior leader of the ISIS-K in Afghanistan, were recognised as Specially Designated Global Terrorists (SDGTs) by the US State Department in November 2021, three months after the Abbey Gate attack.[45] The US had also announced an award of $10 million for information on Ghafari's whereabouts. It was in order to find him that the US apparently carried out a drone attack on 29 August 2021, three days after the Abbey Gate bombing.

In June 2023, Voice of America (VoA) reported that Muhajir had been killed in Kabul in an intelligence-led

EPILOGUE 191

operation in Kunar province by the Taliban. The development, first reported by the American broadcaster, was confirmed by Taliban sources as well as Pakistani intelligence officials. In fact, the Taliban spokesperson Mujahid had claimed, post its takeover of Afghanistan, that the outfit had jailed around 1,700 ISIS-K operatives while killing roughly 1,100. But this was not validated by the US authorities.[46] Subsequently, in July that year, a report by the United Nations Security Council (UNSC) expressed doubts over the killing of Ghafari. The UNSC said in its report:

> Currently, the [ISIS-K] has emerged as the most serious terrorist threat in Afghanistan and the wider region. The group has reportedly increased its operational capabilities inside Afghanistan, with fighters and family members estimated at 4,000 to 6,000 individuals. Sanaullah Ghafari (alias Shahab al-Muhajir) is viewed by some Member States as the most ambitious leader of ISIL-K. One Member State reported that Ghafari was killed in Afghanistan in June. That remains to be confirmed. Mawlawi Rajab is the leader of external operations for [ISIS-K] ... [ISIS-K] is becoming more sophisticated in its attacks against both the Taliban as well as international targets. The group was reportedly focused on a strategy of carrying out high-profile attacks to undermine the Taliban's ability to provide security. Overall, ISIL-K attacks demonstrated strong operational capability involving reconnoitre, coordination, communication, planning and execution. According to some Member States, attacks against high-profile Taliban figures in Balkh, Badakhshan and Baghlan Provinces raised ISIL-K morale and boosted recruitment.[47]

The Dystopian World of the Afghan Diaspora

As the world continues to face crisis after crisis – the latest being the ongoing Russia–Ukraine war, which began in February 2022 – it is paying much less attention to the cause of Afghanistan. The Afghan diaspora continues to live in a dystopian world, no matter whether they are in the US, the UK or Canada, countries where there is the maximum concentration of Afghan nationals. Those who could not afford to make it to a Western country ended up in Pakistan, Iran, Tajikistan, Uzbekistan and Turkey to rebuild their lives. Being victims of big power play and large-scale wars, Afghans have always practised what is known as group migration. Conflict has been among the topmost reasons why millions of Afghans have been forced to leave their homes and their country. Other sociocultural factors have played a minimal role in their movement. The largest migrations from Afghanistan have always been involuntary since the beginning of the twentieth century, being mostly the result of government collapse.[48] However, somehow Afghanistan's diaspora has continued to promote the cause of peace and stability back home, even from the comfort of their host countries. The Afghan people overseas continue to fight for and dream of an Afghanistan where there are no more wars and it is back to the heady days when women roamed freely on the streets and there was no fear of bomb blasts under the Republic. It also needs to be noted here that the Afghan diaspora consists of former bureaucrats, political leaders, civil rights activists and academicians who can make a significant economic and political impact in Afghanistan.

However, the people of the diaspora are somewhat different from the refugees. People migrating from a war zone to another country generally enter the territory of the host country as refugees. And slowly, when they build their lives and careers, they take on the role of a diaspora, but a diaspora that has no home to go back to. According to a report released by the UNHCR in July 2023, there are currently more than 8 million Afghans who have been driven out of their homes or their country on account of conflict, violence and poverty. At least 3.2 million Afghans are displaced within their own country. As the humanitarian crisis continues, the resilience of Afghans and their host communities is being stretched to the limit. Afghan refugees constitute the third-largest displaced population in the world, after Syrian and Ukrainian refugees. In 2023, there were at least 8.2 million Afghans hosted across 103 different countries. A vast majority is living in Pakistan and Iran. Over 70 per cent of those in need of support are women and children.

The US has a long history of welcoming refugees, including Afghan refugees. Some of the Afghan nationals who have been resettled here served as translators or interpreters during the US mission in Afghanistan. Due to their employment with the US government, many faced serious threats to their safety following the Taliban takeover of Kabul. They have come to the US seeking safety for themselves and their families and have been resettled in communities where they are now thriving.[49]

ACKNOWLEDGEMENTS

The book is an outcome of a DM from Prerna Vohra, who was then associated with Bloomsbury, while I was still in Afghanistan covering the NATO troops' withdrawal at the end of the twenty-year-long war started by the US. As luck would have it, the assignment also turned out to be one where I covered the comeback of the Taliban as Afghanistan collapsed in a matter of hours. I loved how passionate Prerna was about geopolitics just as I am. It made me stay with Bloomsbury despite other options that presented themselves after I came back to India.

Bloomsbury's approach was utterly professional from day one. It is not an easy task for an active journalist, who is dishing out stories – breaking, features and routine – almost on a daily basis, to write a book. But Bloomsbury was extremely patient with me and allowed me to write the book the way I wanted to tell my story to the world. My sincere thanks to R. Sivapriya and the team at Bloomsbury India. Sivapriya was kind enough to understand the challenges I faced both personally and professionally during this period. But most importantly, she was willing to hear my story, of my coverage in Afghanistan and her words 'You have a distinct voice and the story needs to be told' encouraged me to carry on. I am also extremely indebted and grateful to Editor-in-Chief Krishan Chopra, who despite his busy schedule picked up my calls and pushed me to write. I sincerely thank each editor on the team who worked on this true account of what happened in Afghanistan in August 2021.

As I began to write the book, in September 2021, the Taliban took the most regressive decision of not allowing education for girls. The following year, the fundamentalist group banned women from universities in Afghanistan, triggering international condemnation even as the economy began to collapse and hunger saw a spike across the country. Although countries refused to recognise the Taliban officially, they, including the US, began dealing with the new regime in Kabul by deploying diplomats designated as 'Special Envoy for Afghanistan'.

Despite having two major stints in the corporate world with lucrative salaries, I always came back to journalism as it was writing that brought the best in me. I am eternally thankful to my husband, Shome Basu, for always having my back, for managing my crazy writing schedule while my mother-in-law fell ill. She passed away at the beginning of this year but I find solace in the fact that she was able to see the final manuscript when it was finished by December 2023. She was always keen to hear stories of my coverage of various places. But she was extra interested in my assignment in Afghanistan. While she was also worried about my safety, not once did she discourage me from taking up the task.

ACKNOWLEDGEMENTS 197

I am forever grateful to my mother, the most important pillar of my life. Whatever I am today is because of her dedication and motivation. I am most thankful to my brother, Anirban, who has always ensured that he fills up the vacuum that was created after our father passed away a decade ago. My father, Arunabha Basu, had been a topper all his life. He always taught me and my brother to do whatever we do in life with utmost honesty. Today, as a journalist, I realise how important it is to be honest. He tried to coax me to write a book. I am sure he is elated now.

This book would not have happened had the editor-in-chief of ThePrint, Shekhar Gupta, and the then managing editor Y.P. Rajesh not agreed to my request to send me to Afghanistan. They trusted me wholeheartedly and provided me with everything I wanted that helped me conduct my work smoothly. I am indebted to Sanghamitra Mazumdar, editor (digital), ABP (Ananda Bazar Patrika) Live – English, and Tushar Banerjee, vice president – digital content and business strategy, ABP Network.

This acknowledgement will not be complete if I do not offer my sincere and heartfelt gratitude to some extremely kind-hearted former diplomats and intelligence officials, who have been there, done that and still feel passionately about the developments in Afghanistan: Anand Arni, Rakesh Sood, Shyam Saran, M.K. Bhadrakumar, Kanwal Sibal and many more whom I cannot name but they know who they are.

ACKNOWLEDGEMENTS

I especially acknowledge my Afghan and other South Asian friends – Malik, Murtaza, Haroon, Iqbal, Mansoor, Frohar, Azad, Mahboba, Farkhunda, Gul, Nisar, Naeem and many others, who have all contributed to this book.

I also need to mention here two extremely kindhearted souls, my son's 2021 class teachers Nidhi ma'am and Tripti ma'am for taking care of my son's studies and caring for him while I was away for this important assignment.

My sincere gratitude to former Indian Army chief General M.M. Naravane and A.S. Dulat, the former chief of R&AW and former special director of the Intelligence Bureau.

Last but not least, a big thank you to my colleagues at ThePrint and ABP Network. And a very special mention to those who amplified my work by offering me their platforms. Thank you Priya Sahgal, Parikshit Luthra, Sahil Makkar and Yamini Pustake Bhalerao.

If I have forgotten someone, please know it is not intentional.

NOTES

CHAPTER 1 LANDING IN KABUL AND A NEAR ARREST: WELCOME TO AFGHANISTAN!

1 https://theprint.in/diplomacy/india-prepares-contingencyplan-as-taliban-gain-ground-evacuates-staff-from-kandaharconsulate/693787/

2 Press release issued by the Indian Consulate General in Kandahar on 27 April. https://cgi.gov.in/kandahar/?12787?000

3 https://www.hindustantimes.com/opinion/in-afghanistanhow-india-missed-the-bus-101626793295492.html

4 https://www.washingtonpost.com/national-security/afghan-government-could-fall-within-six-months-ofus-military-withdrawal-new-intelligence-assessmentsays/2021/06/24/42375b14-d52c-11eb-baed-4abcfa380a17_story.html

5 https://www.aljazeera.com/news/2021/8/11/afghancapital-could-fall-to-taliban-within-90-days-us-intel

6 https://www.reuters.com/world/asia-pacific/taliban-capturegovernment-buildings-afghan-city-kunduz-2021-08-08/

7 https://www.npr.org/2021/09/03/1033966153/afghanistantaliban-panjshir-resistance

CHAPTER 2 POUNDING THE STREETS OF KABUL

1 https://www.aljazeera.com/news/2021/8/9/taliban-captures-more-provincial-capitals-afghanistan

2 https://www.youtube.com/watch?v=PRdzAj19yms

3 https://www.pmindia.gov.in/en/news_updates/signing-ceremony-of-mou-for-the-construction-of-the-lalandar-shatoot-dam-in-afghanistan/

4 https://www.newdelhi.mfa.af/en/news/foreign-minister-meets-former-indian-ambassadors-to-kabul.html

5 https://www.aljazeera.com/news/2021/8/10/us-envoy-indoha-to-press-taliban-for-end-to-offensive

200 NOTES

6 https://theprint.in/diplomacy/afghan-leader-who-shot-dead-terrorists-to-save-indians-now-seeks-delhi-help-in-peace-talks/529727/

7 https://www.bbc.com/news/world-asia-58142983

CHAPTER 3 IN MAZAR, AS INDIA SHUTS ITS LAST CONSULATE AND THE TALIBAN ADVANCES

1 https://www.theguardian.com/global-development/2021/sep/20/its-heartbreaking-steve-mccurry-on-afghan-girl-a-portrait-of-past-and-present

CHAPTER 4 MAZAR, FREE AND BEAUTIFUL: THE TALIBAN DID NOT RUN IT OVER

1 https://www.dodig.mil/In-the-Spotlight/Article/3129145/lead-inspector-general-for-operation-enduring-sentinel-and-operation-freedoms-s/

CHAPTER 5 KABUL: GROWING EERIER DAY BY DAY

1 https://www.aljazeera.com/news/2021/8/12/afghanistanoffer-power-sharing-taliban-official

2 https://abcnews.go.com/Politics/us-diplomats-warnedafghanistans-collapse-dissent-cable-month/story?id=79549635

3 https://www.khaama.com/governor-arrested-after-handingover-ghazni-province-to-taliban-8758475/

4 https://www.reuters.com/world/middle-east/doha-talksafghanistan-end-with-call-accelerated-peace-process-haltattacks-2021-08-12/

5 https://www.newyorker.com/magazine/2021/12/20/thesecret-history-of-the-us-diplomatic-failure-in-afghanistan

6 https://www.wsj.com/articles/afghans-tell-of-executionsforced-marriages-in-taliban-held-areas-116287808207

7 https://twitter.com/USEmbassyKabul/status/1425645725958955012

CHAPTER 6 HAS THE ISLAMIC REPUBLIC OF AFGHANISTAN COLLAPSED?

1 Joseph J. Collins, *The Soviet Invasion of Afghanistan: Methods, Motives and Ramifications*, Lexington Books (1986)

NOTES

2   Yatish Yadav, *RAW: A History of India's Covert Operations*, Westland, 2022.

3   Musa Khan Jalalzai, *Taliban and the Post-Taliban Afghanistan: Terrorism, Al-Qaeda and The Qila-e-Jangi Massacre*, Sang-e-Meel Publication, 2003.

4   https://obamawhitehouse.archives.gov/the-pressoffice/2011/06/22/remarks-president-way-forward-Afghanistan

5   https://www.unhcr.org/news/briefing/2021/7/60ed3ba34/unhcr-warns-imminent-humanitarian-crisis-afghanistan.html

6   https://theprint.in/diplomacy/butcher-of-kabul-gulbuddinhekmatyar-wants-to-be-afghan-president/204135/

7   https://www.washingtonpost.com/world/asia_pacific/afterdecades-as-fugitive-afghan-warlord-gulbuddin-hekmatyarreturns-with-appeal-for-peace/2017/05/04/cc12d1fe-303c-11e7-a335-fa0ae1940305_story.html

CHAPTER 7 MAZAR GONE; CAN KABUL BE FAR BEHIND?

1   https://theprint.in/world/as-mazar-falls-to-taliban looking-back-at-a-city-that-clung-on-to-hope-amid-fear desperation/715446/

2   https://theprint.in/diplomacy/dont-forget-us-as-we-fight taliban-says-afghan-leader-who-thwarted-indian-mission attack/713790/

3   Interview of Alizai: https://www.thedrive.com/the-war-zone/the-last-general-afghanistans-top-commander-on-how-his country-really-fell

4   https://www.youtube.com/watch?v=v9KaQn6AVtw&t=55s

CHAPTER 8 TALIBAN BACK IN KABUL, AND I STRANDED ON THE STREETS

1   https://nsarchive2.gwu.edu/coldwar/interviews/episode-17/brzezinski2.html

2   https://apnews.com/article/afghanistan-biden-politics-united-states-government-james-comer-d75cb39e91b833bc1a2a0fb8bc305e3c

3   A.R. Rowan, *On the Trail of a Lion Ahmed Shah Massoud: Oil, Politics and Terror*, Mosaic Press, 2010.

4   https://www.dodig.mil/In-the-Spotlight/Article/3129145/

NOTES

lead-inspector-general-for-operation-enduring-sentinel-and-operation-freedoms-s/

5   https://foreignpolicy.com/2022/04/28/the-u-s-left-billions-worth-of-weapons-in-afghanistan/

6   https://apnews.com/article/religion-afghanistan-kabul-taliban-22f5107f1dbd19c8605b5b5435a9de54

7   https://www.bbc.com/news/world-asia-58329527

8   https://www.npr.org/2021/09/03/1033966153/afghanistan-taliban-panjshir-resistance

9   https://newrepublic.com/article/73493/our-man-kabul

10 https://twitter.com/KarzaiH/status/1426922752674435084

11 https://www.theatlantic.com/ideas/archive/2021/08/bidens-betrayal-of-afghans-will-live-in-infamy/619764/

12 https://www.theguardian.com/world/2021/aug/15/talibansabdul-ghani-baradar-is-undisputed-victor-of-a-20-year-war

13 The deal between the US and the Taliban signed on 29 February 2020: 'Agreement for Bringing Peace to Afghanistan between the Islamic Emirate of Afghanistan which is not recognized by the US as a state and is known as the Taliban and the US of America'.

CHAPTER 10 BACK HOME WITH A BIT OF AFGHANISTAN IN ME

1   https://www.youtube.com/watch?v=cWFT6jMbUWg

EPILOGUE

1   https://nsarchive2.gwu.edu/coldwar/interviews/episode-17/brzezinski2.html

2   https://apnews.com/article/afghanistan-biden-politics-united-states-government-james-comer-d75cb39e91b833bc1a2a0fb8bc305e3c

3   A.R. Rowan, *On the Trail of a Lion Ahmed Shah Massoud: Oil, Politics and Terror*, Mosaic Press, 2010.

4   https://www.dodig.mil/In-the-Spotlight/Article/3129145/lead-inspector-general-for-operation-enduring-sentinel-and-operation-freedoms-s/

5   https://foreignpolicy.com/2022/04/28/the-u-s-left-billions-worth-of-weapons-in-afghanistan/

6   https://www.bbc.com/news/world-asia-58329527

NOTES

7 https://www.npr.org/2021/09/03/1033966153/afghanistan-taliban-panjshir-resistance

8 https://www.aljazeera.com/news/2021/8/17/transcript-of-talibans-first-press-conference-in-kabul

9 https://www.nytimes.com/2020/02/20/opinion/taliban-afghanistan-war-haqqani.html

10 https://www.constituteproject.org/constitution/Afghanistan_2004

11 https://jia.sipa.columbia.edu/online-articles/archives-interview-lakhdar-brahim

12 https://www.isas.nus.edu.sg/papers/remaking-of-afghanistan-how-the-taliban-are-changing-afghanistans-laws-and-legal-institutions/#_ftn28

13 https://www.voanews.com/a/taliban-say-they-will-use-parts-of-monarchy-constitution-to-run-afghanistan-for-now/6248880.html

14 https://www.crisisgroup.org/asia/south-asia/afghanistan/afghanistans-taliban-expand-their-interim-government

15 https://www.usip.org/publications/2023/08/two-years-under-taliban-afghanistan-terrorist-safe-haven-once-again

16 https://www.wilsoncenter.org/article/zawahiri-killed-us-strike-afghanistan

17 Nayanima Basu, 'Expect India To Take Reasonable Steps: Envoy Mamundzay On Afghanistan Diplomatic Mission Row', ABP Live, 22 May 2023 (Available at https://news.abplive.com/india-at-2047/exclusive-farid-mamundzay-interview-afghanistan-diplomatic-mission-controversy-afghan-ambassador-says-expect-india-to-take-reasonable-steps-1603136).

18 https://news.abplive.com/india-at-2047/afghan-embassy-reopens-india-breaks-silence-says-its-functional-taliban-rule-afghanistan-visa-service-1648520

19 https://www.stimson.org/event/us-policy-toward-afghanistan-a-conversation-with-tom-west/

20 Dr Anwesha Ghosh, 'Is China looking for a greater role in Taliban-ruled Afghanistan?', Indian Council of World Affairs, 20 April 2002 (Available at https://www.icwa.in/show_content.php?lang=1&level=3&ls_id=7256&lid=4908).

21 https://www.china-briefing.com/news/china-and-afghanistan-bilateral-trade-relationship-and-future-outlook/

NOTES

22 https://www.fmprc.gov.cn/eng/zxxx_662805/202203/t20220325_10655541.html

23 Ibid.

24 http://af.china-embassy.gov.cn/eng/dsxx/dszc/

25 https://8am.media/eng/faiz-hameeds-unfulfilled-victory-dreams/

26 https://www.dni.gov/nctc/groups/ttp.html#

27 https://ctc.westpoint.edu/the-tehrik-i-taliban-pakistan-after-the-talibans-afghanistan-takeover/

28 https://www.mei.edu/publications/pakistan-afghan-taliban-relations-face-mounting-challenges

29 https://www.csis.org/analysis/reshaping-us-aid-afghanistan-challenge-lasting-progress

30 https://www.worldbank.org/en/country/afghanistan/overview

31 'Afghanistan Economic Monitor', The World Bank, 31 August 2023.

32 'WFP in Afghanistan forced to drop 10 million people from lifesaving assistance, deepening despair and worry for Afghans', World Food Programme, 5 September 2023.

33 https://abcnews.go.com/Politics/gen-mark-milley-back-us-withdrawal-afghanistan/story?id=103164460

34 https://www.nytimes.com/2021/09/28/us/politics/milley-senate-hearing-afghanistan.html

35 https://www.cfr.org/article/our-biggest-errors-afghanistan-and-what-we-should-learn-them

36 https://thehill-com.cdn.ampproject.org/c/s/thehill.com/opinion/national-security/4176739-how-the-afghanistan-war-commission-aims-to-learn-from-our-longest-conflict/amp/

37 https://edition.cnn.com/interactive/2022/02/kabul-airport-attack-investigation-intl-hnk-dst/index.html

38 https://obamawhitehouse.archives.gov/the-press-office/2011/06/22/remarks-president-way-forward-Afghanistan

39 https://www.sigar.mil/pdf/evaluations/SIGAR-23-16-IP.pdf

40 Ibid.

41 https://www.washingtonpost.com/opinions/2023/09/14/al-qaeda-afghanistan-taliban-destroyed/?pwapi_token=ey-JoeXAiOiJKV1QiLCJhbGciOiJIUzI1NiJ9.eyJyZWFzb24iOi-

NOTES 205

JnaWZoIiwibmJmIjoxNjkoNjYoMDAwLCJpc3MiOiJzdW-
JzY3JpcHRpb25zIiwiZXhwIjoxNjk2MDQ2Mzk5LCJpYXQiO-
jE2OTQ2NjQwMDAsImp0aSI6ImQ2ODFkNjBmLTFlOTY-t
NDkoOC1hYTAyLTQ3ODgyY2YxMDJhOSIsInVybCI6Im-
hodHBzOi8vd3d3Lndhc2hpbmdob25wb3NoLmNvbS9vcGlu-
aW9ucy8yMDIzLzA5LzE0L2FsLXFhZWRhLWFmZ2hhb-
mlzdGFuLXRhbGliYW4tZGVzdHJveWVVkLyJ9.
pUQJH5N3wRhIJV3XsAhgeCaI5tcUDgMuaoLmoM7xV3o

42 https://www.state.gov/meeting-of-u-s-officials-with-taliban-
representatives/

43 Asfandyar Mir, 'The ISIS-K Resurgence', Wilson Center, 8
October 2021 (Available at https://www.wilsoncenter.org/
article/isis-k-resurgence).

44 Ibid.

45 https://www.state.gov/taking-action-against-isis-k/

46 https://www.voanews.com/a/is-k-leader-in-afghanistan-
reported-dead-/7130444.html

47 UNSC Report dated 31 July 2023.

48 https://www.wilsoncenter.org/blog-post/constructive-and-
destructive-role-afghanistans-diaspora

49 'Afghanistan Refugee Crisis Explained', UNHCR report, 18
July 2023.

SOURCES CONSULTED

1. https://nsarchive2.gwu.edu/coldwar/interviews/episode-17/brzezinski2.html
2. https://apnews.com/article/afghanistan-bidenpolitics-united-states-government-james-comerd75cb39e91b833bc1a2a0fb8b-c305e3c
3. A.R. Rowan, *On the Trail of a Lion Ahmed Shah Massoud: Oil, Politics and Terror*, Mosaic Press, 2010.
4. https://www.dodig.mil/In-the-Spotlight/Article/3129145/lead-inspector-general-for-operation-enduring-sentinel-and operation-freedoms-s/
5. https://foreignpolicy.com/2022/04/28/the-u-s-left-billions worth-of-weapons-in-afghanistan/
6. https://www.bbc.com/news/world-asia-58329527
7. Narendra Singh Sarila, *The Untold Story of India's Partition*, HarperCollins, 2009.
8. Ahmed Rashid, *Taliban: The Story of the Afghan Warlords*, Pan, 2001.
9. https://www.aljazeera.com/news/2021/8/11/afghanistan-provinces-city-taliban-ghani-mazar-i-sharif-live-news
10. https://www.youtube.com/watch?v=xWKJD7DBEjw
11. https://www.youtube.com/watch?v=9Y3SruvCO6I
12. https://www.reuters.com/world/middle-east/doha-talks-afghanistan-end-with-call-accelerated-peace-process-halt-attacks-2021-08-12/
13. https://timesofindia.indiatimes.com/videos/international/i-fled-afghanistan-to-avoid-being-hanged-like-najibullah-ashraf-ghani/videoshow/85448834.cms?from=mdr
14. Musa Khan Jalalzai, *Taliban and The Post-Taliban Afghanistan: Terrorism, Al-Qaeda and the Qila-e-Jangi Massacre*, Sang-e-Meel Publication, 2003.

SOURCES CONSULTED

15. Steve Coll, *Ghost Wars: The Secret History Of the CIA, Afghanistan and Bin Laden, From the Soviet Invasion to September 10, 2001,* Penguin Books, 2005.
16. https://www.c-span.org/video/?288675-1/john-burns-war-reporting
17. https://apnews.com/article/religion-afghanistan-kabul-taliban-22f5107f1dbd19c8605b5b5435a9de54
18. https://www.youtube.com/watch?v=BW95blUF4Q4
19. https://theprint.in/world/our-advice-to-taliban-is-avoid-urban-warfare-afghan-ex-pm-hekmatyar-blames-ghani-for-crisis/715960/
20. Steve Coll, *Ghost Wars: The Secret History Of the CIA, Afghanistan and Bin Laden, From the Soviet Invasion to September 10, 2001,* Penguin Books, 2005.
21. https://www.justice.gov/archive/opa/pr/2008/January/08_nsd_029.html

INDEX

A

Abbey Gate incident, 131, 167, 184, 190

Abdullah, Abdullah, 6, 29, 41, 52, 69, 80, 106, 159

Afghan Constitution, 148–150

Afghan diaspora, 192–193

Afghanistan, 1–3, 14, 22–23, 32–34, 59, 139–141, 183–185. *See also* Taliban

America in, 59, 65, 67, 139, 179–191

China ties with, 153, 155–156, 159–165

economy after Taliban takeover, 175–179

ground reporting from, 8

impact of foreign occupation of, 141

inclusive government by Taliban, 150–151, 157, 158

India consulates in, 2, 3, 37

as Islamic Emirate, 147, 162

jihad in, beginning of, 140

Mujahideens in, 34, 63, 91, 140

and Pakistan relationship, 165–175

psyche of people in, 14

Russian invasion of, 34, 61–62

Shah Rukh Khan craze in, 17, 49, 58, 65, 101, 120

soldiers in Afghan forces, 43–45

Soviet withdrawal of troops from, 34, 60–61, 63, 140

Taliban's comeback and takeover of, 1, 11, 20, 22, 29–31, 41, 42, 46, 49, 53–54, 56, 57, 75, 76, 79, 80, 83, 84, 87–89, 98–111, 134, 139, 142–147, 187

terrorist groups in, 151–152

US withdrawal from, 5, 12, 42, 47, 67, 83, 139, 141, 163, 178, 184

Afghanistan embassy, in India, 4, 30, 153–154

Afghanistan Times, 19, 29

Afghanistan War Commission, 181, 183

Afghan National Defense and Security Forces (ANDSF), 185–188, 190

Akhund, Mullah Mohammad Hassan, 147

Akhundzada, Hibatullah, 171

Albania, 107

Alizai, Haibatullah, 83–84

Al-Jazeera, 17, 42, 88

Al-Qaeda, 67, 139, 151–153, 156, 158, 166, 170, 185, 186, 188, 189

America, 5, 59, 65, 67, 139, 179–191. *See also* United States (US)

withdrawal of troops from Afghanistan, 5, 12, 42, 47, 67, 83, 139, 141, 163, 178, 184

Amin, Hafizullah, 62

Amiri, Rina, 188

Amir, Taliban, 149

INDEX

Amir al-Mu'minin, 149
ANDSF. *See* Afghan National
    Defense and Security Forces
    (ANDSF)
Anglo-Afghan wars, 33, 34
Anglo-Russian agreement over
    Pamirs, 1895, 166
Arg Palace, 15, 16, 26, 56, 79, 147
Arni, Anand, 21
Arsalan Guest House, 39
Atmar, Mohammad Haneef, 22,
    23, 103
Austin, Lloyd, 181
Azam, Sultan Aziz, 190

B
Baheer, Obaidullah, 95
Bajauri, Maulvi Faqir Muhammad,
    172
Balkh province, 30, 34–35
Baloch, Babar, 71
Balti, Mufti Khalid, 172
Baradar, Abdul Ghani, 108, 109,
    156, 168
Bearden, Milt, 97
Belt and Road Initiative (BRI), 155,
    159, 160, 163
Biden, Joe, 56, 108, 141, 176, 181, 184
Blinken, Anthony, 152
BRI. *See* Belt and Road Initiative
    (BRI)
Britain, 32, 33
Brzezinski, Zbigniew, 140

C
Carter, Jimmy, 140
Central Asian jihadi units, 151
Chaudhary, Shamila N., 183
China, 3, 24, 56, 139, 153, 155–165
China–Afghanistan–Pakistan
    trilateral cooperation, 160
China–Pakistan Economic
    Corridor (CPEC), 156, 159, 160

CNBC TV18, 7
CNN, 17, 27, 45, 184
Cold War, 34, 61
Comer, James, 141
Czechoslovakia, 140

D
Da'esh, 74
Decker, Karen, 188
Descent into Chaos (Ahmed Rashid),
    149
Digital media journalist, 9
Displacement, 66, 68–71, 193
Doha, intra-Afghan talks in, 5, 56, 69
Donahue, Chris, 140
Dostum, Abdul Rashid, 42, 81
Doval, Ajit, 22, 127
Durand Line, 166, 167
Dustlik (Friendship) Bridge, 82

E
East Turkestan Islamic Movement
    (ETIM), 74, 156, 163

F
Fazlullah, Mullah, 170
Fixer, 36, 107
Friendship Bridge, 82, 140

G
Galwan Valley clash, 23–24
Germany, 153
Ghafari, Sanaullah, 190, 191
Ghani, Ashraf, 4, 12, 15, 22, 25, 26,
    41, 42, 46, 53, 54, 56, 57, 67, 73,
    76, 80, 81, 83, 84, 89, 90, 96, 100,
    103, 106, 168, 175, 186
Ghazni, conquest of, 53, 57
Great Game, 31, 33, 67, 166, 167
The Great Game (Peter Hopkirk), 91
Group migration, 192
Gul Jaan, 66–67
Gupta, Shekhar, 3, 49, 102

INDEX

H

Hamid, Faiz, 17, 167
Hamid Karzai International Airport, 32, 114, 144
Haq, Abul Azad, 4
Haqqani Network, 26, 108–109, 130
Haqqani, Sirajuddin, 109, 147, 152
Hazara communities, 151
Hekmatyar, Gulbuddin, 73, 74, 78, 84, 87, 94–98, 106, 110
Herat, 3, 31, 37, 57, 92
Hezb-e-Islami, 73, 92, 97
Hezb-e-Islami Gulbuddin (HIG), 98

I

Ignatius, David, 188
India, 1–4, 7, 10, 13, 22–24, 26, 37, 47, 54, 130, 139, 143, 150, 153, 154, 157, 158, 164, 168
  consulates in Afghanistan, 3
  Kandahar consulate, closure of, 1, 2
  security threats to, 139
Indian embassy, 20, 24, 53, 72, 76, 116–119, 122, 124–127
Indonesia, 153
Internally displaced people (IDP), 68, 69
Iran, 67, 143, 157, 164, 190, 192, 193
ISI (Inter-Services Intelligence, Pakistan), 2, 17, 97, 167
ISIS-K. *See* Islamic State of Khorasan Province (ISIS-K)
Islamic Emirate of Afghanistan (IEA), 147, 162
Islamic State Khorasan (ISIS-K), 151, 167, 189–191
Israel–Hamas conflict, 156

J

Jackson, Colin F., 183
Jaishankar, S., 22

Jaish-e-Mohammed (JeM), 74
Jalalabad, 3, 31, 37, 61, 79
Japan, 153

K

Kabul, 1, 2, 6, 12, 13, 31, 34, 50, 76, 79
  chaos, terror and torture at airport after Taliban takeover, 114–121, 131–132
  conveyance in, 20–21
  escape from, 113–135
  Indian embassy in, 20, 122, 124
  international journalists at, 30
  life and people in, 14–16, 19–22, 24–28, 52, 54–56, 93
  Taliban at doors of, 88–89
  Taliban taking over, 98–110, 122–124, 130–132
Kakar, Anwaar-ul-Haq, 174
Kam Air flight, 12, 34, 48
Kandahar, 1, 3, 31, 57, 77, 79
  birthplace of Taliban, 2, 77–78
  consulate in, shutting down, 1, 2
  stronghold of Taliban, 2
Karmal, Babrak, 62
Karzai, Hamid, 15, 29, 106, 186
Katju, Vivek, 23
Kazakhstan, 156, 161
Khalilzad, Zalmay, 5
Khan, Imran, 12, 166–168, 173, 175
Khan, Ismail, 57, 60
Khan, Mansoor, 167
Khan, Mohammad Daoud, 62
Khan, Shah Rukh, 17, 49, 58, 65, 101, 120
Khyber Pakhtunkhwa, 169, 174

L

Laden, Osama bin, 152, 156, 170
Laghmani, Daoud, 54
Lalander (Shahtoot) dam, 23
Lashkar-e-Taiba (LeT), 74

INDEX

Lashkar Gah, 64
Li Keqiang, 159
Loya Jirga, 63, 149, 150

M
Malaysia, 153
Mamundzay, Farid, 4, 9, 154
Marx, Karl, 87
Massoud, Ahmad Shah, 15, 143
Mazar, 29, 34–35, 39, 40, 42, 43, 47,
   76, 84, 85, 134
   Blue Mosque in, 37–38
   crowd at airport, 48–49
   environment/people at, 38–39,
      48–50
   Indian consulate in, shutting
      down of, 37
   massacre in 1997, 34–35
   Pul-e-Bukhari area, soldiers at,
      43–46
   Taliban in, 31, 37, 46, 76, 84,
      134
Mehsud, Baitullah, 170
Mehsud, Hakimullah, 170
Milley, Mark, 180–181
Mir, Asfandyar, 151
Mirzakwal, Abdul Satar, 42
Modi, Narendra, 11, 26, 29, 137
Mohammadi, Bismillah Khan, 83
Mohaqiq, Mohammed, 42
Mohib, Hamdullah, 44, 56, 57, 81,
   83, 84, 90, 103
al-Muhajir, Shahab, 190, 191
Mujahideens, 34, 63, 91, 140
Mujahid, Zabihullah, 143, 146, 191
Muttaqi, Amir Khan, 155, 163

N
Najibullah, Mohammed, 63, 90–91
National Reconciliation Policy
   (NRP), 63
National Resistance Front (NRF),
   anti-Taliban, 143, 145, 157

NATO troops, 12, 19, 47, 60, 96,
   107, 134, 144, 185, 187
Nazary, Ali, 145
New York Times, 147
Nizamani, Ubaid Ur Rehman, 173
Noor, Ata Mohammad, 29, 30, 36,
   42, 46–48, 81, 82, 94
Northern Alliance, 41–44, 46, 48
Norway, 153

O
Obama, Barack, 67, 184–186
Omar, Mullah, 77, 78, 109
On War (Carl von Clausewitz), 85

P
Padukone, Deepika, 49, 65
Pakistan, 2, 3, 9–11, 17, 35, 66,
   139–141, 153, 154, 156, 157, 159,
   160, 162, 163, 165–175, 189, 192,
   193
Pakistani Taliban. *See* Tehreek-e-
   Taliban Pakistan (TTP)
Panjshir Valley, 83, 90, 143–145
Pashtun nationalism, 173
Peace talks in Doha, 5–6, 52–53
PenPath (NGO), 142
People's Democratic Party of
   Afghanistan (PDPA), 62
Poland, 29
Poverty, 15, 55, 76, 91, 177, 178, 193
Prasad, Jayant, 23
P2 refugee programme, 107
Public executions, 92, 154

Q
Qadiry, Tahir, 29, 30
Qala-e-Naw, 64
Qatar, 29, 107, 109, 161, 188
Quetta Shura, 170

R
Raghuram, S., 137

INDEX

Rahimi, Salam, 88–89
Rajab, Mawlawi, 190, 191
Rawalpindi, 168
Reagan, Ronald, 97
Roberts, Frederick, 33
Robinson, Linda, 182
Russia, 32–34, 61, 90, 140, 143, 156, 161, 164, 166
Russia–Ukraine war, 45, 61, 156, 157, 192

S
Salahudin, Maulawi Rajab, 190
Saleh, Amrullah, 83, 90
Saran, Shyam, 7
Saudi Arabia, 140, 142, 153, 154
Security threats, 139
Serena hotel, Kabul, 17–18, 20, 21, 26–28, 55, 60, 64, 74, 76, 77, 86–89, 100–104, 108, 109, 113, 136, 167
Serena swagger, 168
Shaheen, Suhail, 73, 124
Shah, Mohammad Zahir, 62, 150
Sharif, Shahbaz, 173
Shehr-e-Naw camp site, 68, 70
SheThePeople, 7
Shura, 170
Siddiqui, Danish, 4
Sinha, Amar, 23
Sood, Rakesh, 23
South Asia, instability in, 141
Special immigrant visas (SIVs), 107, 133
Special Inspector General for Afghanistan Reconstruction (SIGAR), 187
Specially Designated Global Terrorists (SDGT), 190
Sullivan, Jake, 127

T
Taiwan, 163

Tajikistan, 161, 164, 190, 192
Taliban, 1–6, 29, 34–37, 42, 43, 54, 57–59, 67, 74, 77, 90, 139, 149–158, 176, 179–180, 184, 185, 188, 191. *See also* Afghanistan
China engagement with, 155–156, 159–165
coming back to power in Afghanistan, 1, 11, 20, 22, 29–31, 41, 42, 46, 49, 53–54, 56, 57, 75, 76, 79, 80, 83, 84, 87–89, 98–111, 134, 139, 142–147, 187
de facto recognition to, 155–156
Ghazni, conquest of, 53
Indian journalist, killing of, 4–5
Pakistan and TTP, relationship with, 175
Russia engagement with, 156, 157
US engagement with, 158
Taliban 2.0, 59, 106
Taliban (Ahmed Rashid), 120
Tandon, Rudrendra, 25, 137
Taraki, Nur M., 62
Tehreek-e-Taliban Pakistan (TTP), 151, 165–166, 168–172, 174, 189
The Audacity of Hope: Thoughts on Reclaiming the American Dream (Barack Obama), 67
TOLO News, 60, 68
Trump, Donald, 109, 147, 182, 184
TTP. *See* Tehreek-e-Taliban Pakistan (TTP)
Turabi, Mullah Nooruddin, 92
Turkey, 23, 48, 117, 153, 156, 192
Turkmenistan, 161, 164

U
Uighur militants, 156, 163
United Arab Emirates (UAE), 57, 142, 153, 154

INDEX

United Nations High
Commissioner for Refugees
(UNHCR), 71, 193
United Nations Security Council
(UNSC), 191
United States (US), 5, 32, 34, 53,
56–58, 67, 83, 96–98, 107, 109,
127, 131, 132, 134, 139–142, 145,
147, 148,152, 153, 156, 158, 160,
162, 168, 170, 172, 174, 176,
180–190, 193
US Institute of Peace (USIP), 151
Uzbekistan, 30, 82, 140, 156, 161,
164, 190, 192

V
Voice of America (VoA), 190

W
Wakhan Corridor, 162
Wali, Mufti Noor, 171
Wall Street Journal, 57
Wang Yi, 155, 156, 161, 163

Ward, Clarissa, 45
Washington Post, 188
Wesa, Matiullah, 142–143
West, Thomas, 158, 188
White flags *(Shahadas)*, 102, 145
Wilson, Ross, 53
Women education, 106, 142, 157,
174, 180
World Bank, 176, 177
World Food Programme (WFP),
178–179

X
Xi Jinping, 155, 160

Y
Yousafzai, Malala, 170

Z
al-Zawahiri, Ayman, 151–153, 183
Zero Units, 84
Zhao Sheng, 164

ABOUT THE AUTHOR

Nayanima Basu is a New Delhi-based journalist covering foreign policy and strategic and security affairs with nearly two decades of experience. A major in history from the University of Delhi, Nayanima has been professionally associated with several media organisations such as the IANS (Indo-Asian News Service), *Business Standard*, The Hindu Group, ThePrint and ABP Network.

She has covered a wide range of stories such as the assassination of former Pakistan prime minister Benazir Bhutto, India's crucial years at the World Trade Organization (WTO), the global financial recession, India's evolving ties with its difficult neighbours like Pakistan and China, bilateral and multilateral summits and many other stories from conflict zones. In the course of her reportage, she has interviewed several key Indian and international political and military figures.

Writing has always appealed to Nayanima more than facing the camera. She believes journalism is about going on the ground and showcasing authentic voices by way of analytical and long-form reports. That is why she has travelled far and wide, from the US to Russia, Laos to Saudi Arabia, and Iran to Bangladesh. Nayanima was one of the few Indian journalists who covered the return of the Taliban in Afghanistan in August 2021.

She has also worked for multinational organisations like General Electric and the US–India Business Council, which has given her a deep understanding of how the world of business and finance is governed and run.

Nayanima lives in Noida, Uttar Pradesh, with her husband and son.